MW01025702

Q & As

FOR THE

PMBOK®

GUIDE

SIXTH EDITION

Contributors:

Ray Alton, PMP
Frank T. Anbari, PhD, PMP
Nicholas Holdcraft, PMI-ACP, PMP, PgMP, PfMP
Jack Hseih, PMI-PBA, PMP, PgMP, PfMP
Anthony Johnson, PMP, PgMP, PfMP
Te Wu, PMP, PgMP, PfMP
Russel Souza, MBA, PMP

Library of Congress Cataloging-in-Publication Data is on file with the U.S. Copyright O

Q & As for the PMBOK® Guide Sixth Edition

ISBN: 978-1-62825-461-7

Published by: Project Management Institute, Inc.
                    14 Campus Boulevard
                    Newtown Square, Pennsylvania 19073-3299 USA
                    Phone: +1 610 356 4600
                    Fax: +1 610 482 9971
                    Email: customercare@pmi.org
                    Internet: PMI.org

To inquire about discounts for resale or educational purposes, please
contact the PMI Book Service Center.

        PMI Book Service Center
        P.O. Box 932683, Atlanta, GA 31193-2683 USA
        Phone: +1 866 276 4764 (within the U.S. or Canada) or
        +1 770 280 4129 (globally)
        Fax: +1 770 280 4113
        Email: info@bookorders.pmi.org

10 9 8

Table of Contents

PREFACE   v

QUESTIONS

    Section 1: Introduction   1

    Section 2: The Environment in Which
           Projects Operate   11

    Section 3: The Role of the Project Manager   18

    Section 4: Project Integration Management   25

    Section 5: Project Scope Management   32

    Section 6: Project Schedule Management   41

    Section 7: Project Cost Management   53

    Section 8: Project Quality Management   67

    Section 9: Project Resource Management   76

    Section 10: Project Communications
            Management   86

    Section 11: Project Risk Management   92

    Section 12: Project Procurement
            Management   102

    Section 13: Project Stakeholder
            Management   110

Appendix X3

    Agile, Iterative, Adaptive, and Hybrid
    Project Environments   **117**

Appendix X4

    Summary of Key Concepts for
    Knowledge Areas   **119**

Appendix X5

    Summary of Tailoring Considerations
    for Knowledge Areas   **129**

Glossary   **132**

ANSWERS

Section 1: Introduction   147

Section 2: The Environment in Which
           Projects Operate   160

Section 3: The Role of the Project Manager   171

Section 4: Project Integration Management   183

Section 5: Project Scope Management   198

Section 6: Project Schedule Management   209

Section 7: Project Cost Management   232

Section 8: Project Quality Management   257

Section 9: Project Resource Management   268

Section 10: Project Communications
            Management   281

Section 11: Project Risk Management   290

Section 12: Project Procurement
            Management   305

Section 13: Project Stakeholder
            Management   317

Appendix X3

Agile, Iterative, Adaptive, and Hybrid
Project Environments   **328**

Appendix X4

Summary of Key Concepts for
Knowledge Areas   **332**

Appendix X5

Summary of Tailoring Considerations for
Knowledge Areas   **342**

Glossary   **346**

Preface

In the rapidly growing, fast-changing, and highly competitive world of project management, more and more professionals are recognizing the importance of developing a deeper understanding of the generally accepted knowledge and practice of the project management profession. *Q & As for the PMBOK® Guide Sixth Edition* facilitates this goal by offering multiple-choice questions and answers that cover key themes and concepts of project management. This helpful book addresses the project management Knowledge Areas and processes of *A Guide to the Project Management Body of Knowledge (PMBOK® Guide)* – Sixth Edition, the Project Management Institute's (PMI) global standard and body of knowledge. Answers are provided in the back of the book and include references and excerpted text from the *PMBOK® Guide* – Sixth Edition to enhance the reader's breadth and depth of knowledge. The handy, pocket-size *Q & As for the PMBOK® Guide Sixth Edition* makes it convenient to refer to the information in *The Guide* anytime, anywhere.

Q & As
FOR THE
PMBOK® GUIDE
SIXTH EDITION
Questions

Introduction
(Section 1 of the *PMBOK® Guide*)

1. A project is:

A. A set of sequential activities performed in a process or system.

B. A revenue-generating activity that needs to be accomplished while achieving customer satisfaction.

C. An ongoing endeavor undertaken to meet customer or market requirements.

D. A temporary endeavor undertaken to create a unique product, service, or result.

2. Project management is:

A. The integration of the critical path method and the Earned Value Management system.

B. The application of knowledge, skills, tools, and techniques to project activities to meet the project requirements.

C. The application of knowledge, skills, wisdom, science, and art to organizational activities to achieve operational excellence.

D. A subset of most engineering and other technical disciplines.

3. Portfolio management refers to:

A. Managing various contents of the project file.

B. Managing the levels of financial authority to facilitate project decision making.

C. The centralized management of one or more portfolios to achieve strategic objectives.

D. Applying resource-leveling heuristics across all the organization's projects to achieve the organization's strategic objectives.

4. All of the following are questions that the key stakeholders and project managers should answer to develop the project success measures EXCEPT:

A. What does success look like for the project?

B. How will success be measured?

C. What are the communication requirements?

D. What factors may impact success?

5. A program is a:

A. Group of related tasks lasting one year or less.

B. Group of related projects, subsidiary programs, and program activities managed in a coordinated manner.

C. Large projects with significant cost and resource requirements.

D Sequence of activities constituting a major project.

6. All of the following are true about projects and operations EXCEPT:

A. Operations are ongoing endeavors that produce repetitive outputs, with resources assigned to do basically the same set of tasks according to the standards institutionalized in a product life cycle, whereas projects are temporary endeavors.

B. Projects require project management activities and skill sets, whereas operations require business process management, operations management activities, and skill sets.

C. Projects can intersect with operations at various points during the product life cycle. At each point, deliverables and knowledge are transferred between the project and operations for implementation of the delivered work.

D. Because of their temporary nature, projects cannot help achieve an organization's long-term goals. Therefore, strategic activities in the organization can be generally addressed within the organization's normal operations.

7. Your job responsibility is to align components (projects, programs, or related operations) to the organizational strategy, organized into portfolios or subsidiary portfolios to optimize project or program objectives, dependencies, costs, timelines, benefits, resources, and risks. This is known as:

A. Components management.

B. Process management.

C. Program management.

D. Portfolio management.

8. The *PMBOK® Guide* is the standard for:

A. Managing all projects all of the time.

B. Managing all projects most of the time.

C. Managing most projects most of the time.

D. Managing some projects some of the time.

9. The collection of generally sequential and sometimes overlapping project phases, whose name and number are determined by the management and control needs of the organization or organizations involved in the project, is known as the:

A. Project waterfall.

B. Project life cycle.

C. Project life stages.

D. Project Management Process Groups.

10. **All of the following are true about project phases and the project life cycle EXCEPT:**

A. Stakeholder influences, risk, and uncertainty are greatest at the start of the project. These factors decrease over the life of the project.

B. The ability to influence the final characteristics of the project's product, without significantly impacting cost, is highest at the start of the project and decreases as the project progresses toward completion.

C. The cost of changes and correcting errors typically increases substantially as the project approaches completion.

D. Cost and staffing levels are generally steady throughout the project life cycle.

11. **All of the following statements about the project life cycle and the product life cycle are true EXCEPT:**

A. In the project predictive life cycle, the project scope and the time and cost required to deliver that scope are determined as early in the project life cycle as practically possible.

B. In the project iterative and incremental life cycles, project phases intentionally repeat one or more project activities as the project team's understanding of the product increases.

C. The product life cycle is the series of phases that represent the evolution of a product, from concept through delivery, growth, maturity, and to retirement.

D. The product life cycle is contained within the predictive project life cycle.

12. **You are managing a project in which you intend to respond to high levels of change and ongoing stakeholder involvement. The most suitable project life cycle for your project is the:**

A. Predictive life cycle.

B. Adaptive life cycle.

C. Waterfall life cycle.

D. Configuration management life cycle.

13. **The five Project Management Process Groups are:**

   A. Planning, Checking, Directing, Monitoring, and Recording.

   B. Initiating, Planning, Executing, Monitoring and Controlling, and Closing.

   C. Planning, Executing, Directing, Closing, and Commissioning.

   D. Initiating, Executing, Monitoring, Evaluating, and Closing.

14. **Project Management Processes:**

   A. May be overlapping activities that occur throughout the project.

   B. May be overlapping activities that generally occur at the same level of intensity within each phase of the project.

   C. Are generally discrete, one-time events.

   D. Are discrete, repetitive events that occur generally at the same level of intensity throughout each phase of the project.

15. The linkages between project management processes are best described by the following:

A. The work breakdown structure links processes.

B. Processes are linked by their planned objectives—the summary objective of one often becomes the detailed action plan for another within the project, subproject, or project phase.

C. Processes are linked by the outputs that are produced—the output of one process generally becomes an input to another process or is a deliverable of the project, subproject, or project phase.

D. There are no significant links between discrete processes.

16. For a project to be successful, the project should generally achieve all of the following EXCEPT:

A. Achieving stakeholder satisfaction.

B. Striving to obtain acceptable customer/end-user adoption.

C. Appling knowledge, skills, and processes within the Project Management Process Groups uniformly to meet the project objectives.

D. Fulfilling other agreed-upon success measures or criteria.

17. **The project business case is all of the following EXCEPT:**

   A. Documented economic feasibility study used to establish the validity of the benefits of a selected component lacking sufficient definition and that is used as a basis for the authorization of further project management activities.

   B. A document that lists the objectives and reasons for project initiation.

   C. A document that serves as an important input to the project initiation and is seldom used after the project is approved.

   D. An important document that may result in a go/no-go decision for the project.

18. **The key elements of the benefits management plan are all of the following EXCEPT:**

   A. Work Breakdown Structure.

   B. Benefits owner.

   C. Assumptions.

   D. Strategic alignment.

19. **A significant amount of data is collected and analyzed throughout the project. All of the following are examples of project data and information EXCEPT:**

    A. Work performance data.

    B. Work performance analysis.

    C. Work performance information.

    D. Work performance reports.

20. **Project tailoring is an important consideration for most projects. Which of the following is the least likely project consideration?**

    A. Project manager's skills and competency.

    B. Each project is unique.

    C. Addressing competing constraints.

    D. Level of project governance varies.

The Environment in Which Projects Operate

(Section 2 of the *PMBOK® Guide*)

21. Enterprise environmental factors refer to both internal and external environmental factors that surround or influence a project's success. All of the following are true about these factors EXCEPT:

A. Enterprise environmental factors include organizational culture, structure, and processes.

B. Enterprise environmental factors include government or industry standards, such as regulatory agency regulations, codes of conduct, product standards, quality standards, and workmanship standards.

C. Enterprise environmental factors include information technology software (e.g., an automated tool, such as a scheduling software tool, a configuration management system, an information collection and distribution system, or web interfaces to other online automated systems).

D. Enterprise environmental factors exclude personnel administration functions (e.g., staffing and retention guidelines, employee performance reviews and training records, and time tracking) because these are considered to be functions of the human resources department.

22. The types of project management office (PMO) structures in organizations include all of the following EXCEPT:

A. Supportive PMOs that provide a consultative role to projects by supplying templates, best practices, training, access to information, and lessons learned from other projects.

B. Controlling PMOs that provide support and require compliance through various means.

C. Harmonizing PMOs that strive to reduce conflict and improve harmony among project team members.

D. Directive PMOs that take control of the projects by directly managing the projects.

23. A primary function of a project management office (PMO) is to support project managers in a variety of ways, which may include all of the following EXCEPT:

A. Intervening in project execution directly and without involving the project manager.

B. Managing shared resources across all projects administered by the PMO.

C. Identifying and developing project management methodology, best practices, and standards.

D. Coaching, mentoring, training, and oversight.

24. All of the following are potential information in organizational knowledge repositories EXCEPT:

A. Metrics used to collect and make available measurement data on processes and products.

B. Configuration management.

C. Tacit knowledge of previous projects such as project performance data and lessons learned.

D. Issue and defect management data.

25. All of the following are external environmental factors EXCEPT:

A. Legal restrictions.

B. Organizational values and principles.

C. Competitive movements.

D. Economic conditions.

26. **Organizational process assets (OPAs) influence the management of projects. Which one of the following best describes the important categories of OPAs?**

    A. Organizational knowledge bases and processes.

    B. Processes, policies, procedures, tools, and techniques.

    C. Organizational knowledge bases, processes, policies, and procedures.

    D. Organizational knowledge bases, tools, and techniques.

27. **The organization's processes and procedures for conducting project work during project initiation and planning include all of the following EXCEPT:**

    A. Preapproved supplier list.

    B. Traceability matrices.

    C. Tailoring guidelines for project management processes and procedures.

    D. Product and project life cycles, and methods and procedures.

28. **The organization's processes and procedures for conducting project work during Executing, Monitoring, and Controlling include all of the following EXCEPT:**

A. Change control procedure.

B. Issue and defect management procedures.

C. Resource availability control and assignment management.

D. Project closing guidelines.

29. **Projects operate within the constraints imposed by the organization through their structure and governance framework. The system factors include all of the following EXCEPT:**

A. Management elements.

B. Governance framework.

C. Organizational structure types.

D. Project management processes.

30. **The interaction of the various system components creates the organizational culture and capabilities that are important for projects. Which role is typically responsible for establishing the system?**

    A. Organization's management.

    B. Project sponsor.

    C. Project manager.

    D. Project team.

31. **Governance is the framework within which authority is exercised in organizations. This framework includes all of the following components EXCEPT:**

    A. Rules.

    B. Policies.

    C. Techniques.

    D. Relationships.

32. Which of the following best describe management elements?

A. Management elements are the components that comprise the key functions or principles of general management in the organization.

B. Management elements are the project management principles that guide how projects are executed in the organization.

C. Management elements are established by PMOs to guide project implementation.

D. Management elements are influenced by the governance framework, established for effective implementation of projects.

The Role of the Project Manager
(Section 3 of the *PMBOK® Guide*)

33. All of the following are generally true about leadership in a project environment EXCEPT:

A. It involves focusing the efforts of a group of people toward a common goal and enabling them to work as a team.

B It is the ability to get things done through others.

C. Respect and trust, rather than fear and submission, are the key elements of effective leadership.

D. Although important throughout all project phases, effective leadership is critical during the Closing phase of a project when the emphasis is on stakeholder acceptance of the project.

34. Project managers spend the majority of their time communicating with team members and other project stakeholders. To communicate effectively, the project manager should generally perform all of the following EXCEPT:

A. Calculating the potential number of communication channels accurately.

B. Developing finely tuned skills using multiple methods of communication.

C. Incorporating feedback channels.

D. Seeking to understand project stakeholders' communication needs.

35. All of the following are components of culture EXCEPT:

A. Values.

B. Norms.

C. Intelligence.

D. Beliefs.

36. When performing integration on the project, the role of the project manager is:

A. To work with the project sponsor to understand the strategic objectives and ensure the alignment of the project objectives and results with those of the project and business area.

B. To perform all of the work that is required to get the project approved and baselined for communication to the team.

C. To complete the project charter and seek formal approval from the sponsor of the project.

D. To involve the team in group activities to facilitate teamwork, which builds an integrated project organizational structure.

37. Performing integration is a cornerstone skill for all project managers; the following describe the three different levels of performing integration EXCEPT:

A. Cognitive level.

B. Process level.

C. Complexity level.

D. Context level.

38. Complexity within projects is a result of many different organizational behaviors; the dimensions of complexity include all of the following EXCEPT:

A. System behavior.

B. Human behavior.

C. Ambiguity.

D. Process behavior.

39. Which of the following is least likely to be a project manager's role?

A. Evaluation and analysis of project-related activities prior to project initiation.

B. Consulting with business leaders on advancing strategic objectives.

C. Assisting in business analysis, business case development, and aspects of portfolio management for a project.

D. Ensuring that organizations are operating efficiently.

40. Which of the following is least likely to be within the project manager's sphere of influence?

A. Government.

B. Project team.

C. Sponsors.

D. Customers.

41. The following are all key competencies of a project manager EXCEPT:

A. Technical project management.

B. Operational management.

C. Leadership.

D. Strategic management.

42. The following are all key differences between management and leadership EXCEPT:

A. Directing vs. influencing.

B. Focus on systems vs. focus on relationships.

C. Accept status quo vs. challenge status quo.

D. Concentrate on project activities vs. emphasis on results.

43. Leadership and management are ultimately about being able to get things done, and power plays an important part. Which of the following best describe the various forms of power?

A. Positional, referent, personal, cultural, and relational.

B. Positional, personal, relational, guilt-based, informational, and expertise.

C. Referent, personal, expertise, and cultural.

D. Positional and pressure-based.

44. **Personality refers to the individual differences in characteristic patterns of thinking, feeling, and behaving. Which of the following are the least appropriate characteristics for project managers?**

A. Authentic, courteous, creative, cultural, and emotional.

B. Intellectual, managerial, political, service-oriented, and social.

C. Authentic, managerial, service-oriented, social, and system.

D. Complexity, courteous, intellectual, cultural, and managerial.

45. **Project managers exhibit different leadership styles. Which of the following is NOT a leadership style?**

A. Laissez-faire.

B. Motivational.

C. Charismatic.

D. Servant.

46. **Complexity exhibits all of the following characteristics EXCEPT:**

   A. Containing multiple parts.

   B. Containing high-risk parts.

   C. Exhibiting dynamic interactions between the parts.

   D. Exhibiting emergent behavior, which cannot be easily explained as the simple sum of parts.

47. **Project managers are similar to conductors of a large orchestra, EXCEPT:**

   A. They are responsible for the final result of the team.

   B. They communicate with the team.

   C. They need to integrate multiple disciplines.

   D. They need to be an expert or knowledgeable of all aspects of their endeavor.

Project Integration Management
(Section 4 of the *PMBOK® Guide*)

48. Which of the following processes is included in Project Integration Management?

A. Develop project management plan.

B. Control scope definition.

C. Review scope validation.

D. Conduct procurement surveillance.

49. All of the following are characteristics of the project charter EXCEPT:

A. It formally authorizes the existence of a project.

B. Projects are initiated by an entity external to the project. The project initiator or sponsor should be at the level that is appropriate to procure funding and commit resources to the project.

C. It is used primarily to request bids for a project or a specific phase of a project.

D. It provides the project manager with the authority to apply organizational resources to project activities.

50. All of the following are characteristics of the Project Management Information System (PMIS) EXCEPT:

A. Automated gathering and reporting on key performance indicators (KPIs) can be part of this system.

B. It provides access to information technology (IT) software tools, such as scheduling software tools, work authorization systems, and configuration management systems.

C. It is used as part of the Direct and Manage Project Work.

D. It is used by the project manager and the project management team primarily to generate presentations to key stakeholders.

51. Which of the following is NOT true about tools and techniques of Perform Integrated Change Control?

A. They include expert judgment.

B. They include change control meetings.

C. A change control board (CCB) is responsible for meeting and reviewing the change requests and approving, rejecting, or other disposition of those changes.

D. They include project plan updates.

52. You are managing a $10 million project. Which of the following is an acceptable cause for "re-baselining" this project?

A. The client has approved an addition to the scope of the project with a $150,000 budget increase and a two-week extension of the scheduled completion.

B. The contractor's company has instituted a quality assurance program in which it has pledged to spend $1 million during the next year.

C. The productivity in the design department is lower than estimated, which has resulted in 1,000 additional hours over what was budgeted and a forecasted two-week delay of the scheduled completion.

D. The engineering department of the performing organization has converted to a new $250,000 CAD system.

53. Configuration management is focused on:

A. The identification and correction of problems arising in functional areas of project implementation.

B. The specification of both the deliverables and the processes, while change control is focused on identifying, documenting, and approving or rejecting changes to the project documents, deliverables, or baselines.

C. Testing new systems.

D. Identifying, documenting, and controlling changes to the project and the product baselines, while change control is focused on the specifications of both the deliverables and the processes.

54. A change control board (CCB) is:

A. A formally chartered group of stakeholders responsible for ensuring that only a minimal amount of changes occurs on the project.

B. A formal or an informal group of stakeholders that has oversight of project execution.

C. A formally chartered group responsible for reviewing, evaluating, approving, delaying, or rejecting changes to the project, and for recording and communicating such decisions.

D. A dashboard that provides integrated information to help control changes to cost, schedule, and specifications throughout the life of the project.

55. **Some of the configuration management activities included in the Perform Integrated Change Control process include all of the following activities EXCEPT:**

A. Identification and selection of a configuration item to provide the basis for which the product configuration is defined and verified, products and documents are labeled, changes are managed, and accountability is maintained.

B. Monitoring changes in resource-leveling heuristics to ensure efficient resource utilization throughout the life cycle of the project.

C. Configuration status accounting, in which information is recorded and reported as to when appropriate data about the configuration item should be provided.

D. Configuration verification and configuration audits that ensure that the composition of a project's configuration items is correct and that corresponding changes are registered, assessed, approved, tracked, and correctly implemented.

56. **Actions and activities necessary to transfer the project's products, services, or results to the next phase or to production and/or operations are addressed:**

A. As part of the Close Project or Phase process.

B. Following the plan outlined in the Quality Management process.

C. As requested by senior executives.

D. As the last step in project management.

57. **Outputs of the Monitor and Control Project Work process include all of the following EXCEPT:**

   A. Change requests.

   B. Project management plan updates.

   C. Work performance reports.

   D. Final product, service, or result transition.

58. **All of the following are inputs to Manage Project Knowledge EXCEPT:**

   A. Deliverables.

   B. Knowledge management.

   C. Lessons learned register.

   D. Project management plan.

59. **All of the following are Knowledge Management tools and techniques EXCEPT:**

   A. Discussion forums.

   B. Storytelling.

   C. Work shadowing and reverse shadowing.

   D. Regression analysis.

60. Lessons learned documentation generally includes all of the following EXCEPT:

A. The causes of issues.

B. Updates of the statement of work to reflect training and learning requirements.

C. Reasoning behind the corrective action chosen.

D. Other types of lessons learned about communications management.

Project Scope Management
(Section 5 of the *PMBOK® Guide*)

61. All of the following are true about the project scope management plan EXCEPT:

A. It enables the creation of the WBS from the detailed project scope statement.

B. It describes how the scope will be defined, developed, monitored, controlled, and validated.

C. It can be formal or informal, broadly framed or highly detailed, based on the needs of the project.

D. It is not related to the project management plan.

62. **Collect Requirements is the process of determining, documenting, and managing stakeholder needs and requirements to meet project objectives. All of the following are true about this process EXCEPT:**

A. The project's success is directly influenced by active stakeholder involvement in the discovery and decomposition of needs into requirements and by the care taken in determining, documenting, and managing the requirements of the product, service, or result of the project.

B. Requirements become the foundation of the WBS. Cost, schedule, quality planning, and sometimes procurement are all based upon these requirements.

C. The development of requirements begins with an analysis of the information contained in the project charter, the risk register, and the stakeholder engagement plan.

D. Requirements need to be elicited, analyzed, and recorded in enough detail to be included in the scope baseline and to be measured once project execution begins.

63. You are involved in collecting requirements for your project. You are likely to use the stakeholder register for all of the following EXCEPT:

A. Identifying stakeholders who can provide information on the requirements.

B. Capturing major requirements that stakeholders may have for the project.

C. Capturing main expectations that stakeholders may have for the project.

D. Evaluating the product breakdown structure (PBS) associated with each of the key stakeholders.

64. You are developing a document that links product requirements from their origin to the deliverables that satisfy them to help ensure that each requirement adds business value and to manage changes to the product scope. This is known as the:

A. Configuration management system.

B. Business case.

C. New product development matrix.

D. Requirements traceability matrix.

65. An output of the Define Scope process is:

A. Work breakdown structure (WBS).

B. Resource breakdown structure (RBS).

C. Project scope statement.

D. Scope and schedule delays control plan.

66. All of the following are true about the project scope statement EXCEPT:

A. It is an output of the Validate Scope process.

B. It describes, in detail, the project's deliverables and the work required to create those deliverables.

C. It provides a common understanding of the project scope among project stakeholders.

D. It may contain explicit scope exclusions that can assist in managing stakeholder expectations.

67. Which of the following statements is true about the work breakdown structure (WBS)?

A. The WBS is a hierarchical decomposition of the total scope of work to be carried out by the project team to accomplish the project objectives and create the required deliverables.

B. The WBS is a simple list of project activities in chart form.

C. The WBS is the same as the organizational breakdown structure (OBS).

D. The WBS is the bill of materials (BOM) needed to accomplish the project objectives and create the required deliverables.

68. The following is an example of a constraint associated with the project scope that limits the team's options in scope definition:

A. A predefined budget or any imposed dates or schedule milestones that are issued by the customer or performing organization.

B. The threat of a strike by a subcontractor.

C. Existing relationships with sellers, suppliers, or others in the supply chain.

D. The method used to measure project performance.

69. An input to the Define Scope process is:

A. The type of contract detail language.

B. Project charter.

C. Work breakdown structure (WBS).

D. Decomposition.

70. What is the WBS typically used for?

A. To organize and define the total scope of the project.

B. To identify the logical person to be project sponsor.

C. To define the level of reporting that the seller provides the buyer.

D. As a record of when work elements are assigned to individuals.

71. The following is true about the WBS:

A. The WBS is another term for the bar (Gantt) chart.

B. Each descending level of the WBS represents an increasingly detailed definition of the project work.

C. Work not in the WBS is usually defined in the scope statement of the project.

D. The WBS shows only the critical path activities.

72. Which of the following is true about the Validate Scope process?

A. It is the process of formalizing acceptance of the completed project deliverables.

B. It is not necessary if the project completes on time and within budget.

C. It occurs primarily when revisions or changes are made to project scope.

D. Scope validation is primarily concerned with correctness of the deliverables, whereas quality control is primarily concerned with acceptance of the deliverables and meeting the quality requirements specified for the deliverables.

73. You are managing a global project that involves stakeholders in several international locations. You are likely to consult the WBS dictionary to find:

A. The language translation of technical terms used in the project.

B. Detailed deliverable, activity, and scheduling information about each component in the WBS.

C. Information relating the legal constraints of relevant international locations to the development of the WBS.

D. Strengths, weaknesses, opportunities, and threats (SWOT) of key stakeholders and their impact on the WBS.

74. Which of the following is NOT an output of the Control Scope process?

A. Work performance information.

B. Change requests.

C. Project documents updates.

D. Accepted deliverables.

75. All of the following are true about the Control Scope process EXCEPT:

A. Control Scope is the process of monitoring the status of the project and product scope and managing changes to the scope baseline.

B. Control Scope is used to manage the actual changes when they occur and is integrated with the other control processes.

C. Scope changes can be avoided by developing clear and concise specifications and enforcing strict adherence to them.

D. Controlling the project scope ensures that all requested changes and recommended corrective or preventive actions are processed through the Perform Integrated Change Control process.

76. _____ describe capabilities that are temporary and are no longer needed after the new product/service/result is ready.

A. Business requirements

B. Solution requirements

C. Quality requirements

D. Transition requirements

77. Agile scope planning is especially useful when:

A. Solution requirements are emerging all the time.

B. Quality requirements are not stable.

C. Business requirements are not stable.

D. Scope is well understood at the beginning.

Project Schedule Management
(Section 6 of the *PMBOK® Guide*)

78. In rolling wave planning:

A. Focus is maintained on long-term objectives, allowing near-term objectives to be rolled out as part of the ongoing wave of activities.

B. The work to be accomplished in the near term is planned in detail, whereas the work in the future is planned at a higher level.

C. The work far in the future is planned in detail for work packages that are at a low level of the WBS.

D. A wave of detailed activities is planned during strategic planning to ensure that WBS deliverables and project milestones are achieved.

79. The precedence diagramming method (PDM) is:

A. A technique in which activities are represented by nodes and are graphically linked by one or more logical relationships to show the sequence in which the activities are to be performed.

B. A method that uses a probabilistic approach to scheduling project activities.

C. A time-phased graphical representation of the arrow diagramming method (ADM), and shows durations of project activities as well as their dependencies.

D. More accurate than the critical path method for scheduling when there are uncertainties about the durations of project activities.

80. The duration of the activity is affected by all of the following EXCEPT:

A. The estimated activity resource requirements.

B. The types of resources assigned to the activity.

C. The availability of the resources assigned to the activity.

D. Using the precedence diagramming method (PDM) for scheduling activities instead of using the critical path method (CPM).

81. A schedule compression technique used to shorten the schedule duration for the least incremental cost by adding resources is called:

A. Crashing.

B. Program evaluation and review technique (PERT).

C. Precedence diagramming method (PDM).

D. Fast tracking.

82. **The "fast tracking" method of schedule compression involves:**

A. The use of industrial engineering techniques to improve productivity, thereby finishing the project earlier than originally planned.

B. Performing in parallel for at least a portion of their duration activities or phases that are normally done in sequence, which may result in rework and increased risk.

C. Going on a "mandatory overtime schedule" to complete the project on schedule or earlier if possible.

D. Assigning "dedicated teams" to critical path activities to achieve project schedule objectives.

83. **An example of a mandatory dependency is:**

A. A dependency established based on knowledge of best practices within a particular application area.

B. A dependency established based on some unusual aspect of the project where a specific sequence is desired.

C. On a construction project, to erect the superstructure only after the foundation has been built.

D. On a software development project, to start design only after completion and approval of all project requirements.

84. Inputs to the Define Activities process are:

A. Schedule management plan, work breakdown structure, project schedule, and network diagram.

B. Project schedule, resource estimates, progress reports, and change requests.

C. Scope management plan, project network diagram, constraints, and assumptions.

D. Schedule management plan, scope baseline, enterprise environmental factors, and organizational process assets.

85. For project scheduling, bar charts show:

A. The level of effort for an activity.

B. Availability of resources assigned to perform project activities.

C. Activity start and end dates, as well as expected durations.

D. Relative priority of activities.

86. The precedence diagramming method (PDM) shows:

A. Various levels of the work breakdown structure.

B. Activities likely to be involved in project integration and resource allocation processes.

C. The logical relationships that exist between activities.

D. The project completion date based on normal resource availability.

87. The critical path is established by calculating the following dates:

A. Start-to-start, start-to-finish, finish-to-finish, finish-to-start.

B. Early start, early finish, late start, late finish.

C. Predecessor-to-successor, predecessor-to-predecessor, successor-to-successor.

D. Primary-to-secondary, primary-to-finish, secondary-to-secondary, finish-to-finish.

88. All of the following are true about resource leveling EXCEPT:

A. It can be used to keep resource usage at a constant level during certain time periods.

B. It can often cause the original critical path to change.

C. It is used to develop a resource-based WBS.

D. It is a resource optimization technique that can be used to adjust the schedule model due to demand and supply of resources.

89. As one of the tools and techniques of the Sequence Activities process, a lead:

A. Directs a delay in the successor activity.

B. Could be accomplished by a finish-to-start relationship with a delay time.

C. Means that the successor activity cannot start until after the predecessor is completed.

D. Is the amount of time whereby a successor activity can be started before the previous activity is completed.

90. Three-point estimating uses:

A. An optimistic, pessimistic, and most likely estimate to calculate the estimate.

B. The weighted average of optimistic, pessimistic, and most likely estimates to calculate the expected duration of the activity.

C. Dummy activities to represent logic links among three or more activities.

D. Free float instead of total float in the schedule calculations.

91. Analogous duration estimating is:

A. Frequently used to estimate project duration when there is a limited amount of detailed information about the project.

B. A bottom-up estimating technique.

C. Based on multiple duration estimating.

D. Generally more accurate than other duration estimating methods when expert judgment is used.

92. Consider the following three estimates for the duration of an activity:
Optimistic (tO) = 4 weeks
Most likely (tM) = 5 weeks
Pessimistic (tP) = 9 weeks

Using the beta distribution and the three-point estimating approach, the calculated Expected activity duration (tE) is:

A. 4.0 weeks.

B. 4.5 weeks.

C. 5.5 weeks.

D. 6.5 weeks.

93. Consider the following information about the duration of an activity:
Calculated expected (tE) = 5 weeks
Optimistic (tO) = 4 weeks
Pessimistic (tP) = 8 weeks

Using the beta distribution and the three-point estimating approach, the Most likely (tM) activity duration is:

A. 4.0 weeks.

B. 4.5 weeks.

C. 5.0 weeks.

D. 6.0 weeks.

94. **Consider the following three estimates for the duration of an activity:**
    Optimistic (tO) = 6 weeks
    Most likely (tM) = 9 weeks
    Pessimistic (tP) = 15 weeks

    Using the triangular distribution, the calculated Expected activity duration (tE) is:

    A. 10.0 weeks.

    B. 10.5 weeks.

    C. 11.5 weeks.

    D. 12.0 weeks.

95. **An activity in a project network has the following characteristics: ES = 5, EF = 10, and LF = 14. Therefore, LS = _____.**

    A. 9.0 weeks.

    B. 10.0 weeks.

    C. 11.0 weeks.

    D. 12.0 weeks.

96. **An activity in a network has the following characteristics: ES = 12, EF = 22, and LS = 14. ES and LS relate to the beginning of the week, whereas EF relates to the end of the week. The duration of the activity is:**

A. 8.0 weeks.

B. 11.0 weeks.

C. 12.0 weeks.

D. 14.0 weeks.

97. **"Crashing" in schedule management is:**

A. A schedule compression technique used to shorten the schedule duration for the least incremental cost by adding resources.

B. A schedule compression technique in which phases or activities that are normally done in sequence are performed in parallel.

C. The timely input of data to calculate the critical path.

D. Equivalent to minimizing float in the project schedule network.

Consider the following schedule network that shows the activities in your project and their associated durations in days for questions 98–99:

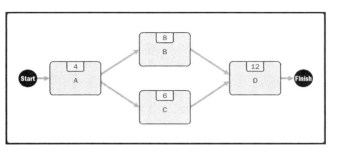

98. The critical path in this network is:

   A. A-B-C.

   B. A-B-D.

   C. A-C-D.

   D. A-B-C-D.

99. The free float for activity C is:

   A. +4.

   B. +2.

   C. 0.

   D. −2.

100. The Control Schedule process for a project:

A. Focuses on starting the project earlier than scheduled to help mitigate schedule risk and to achieve the approved schedule baseline.

B. Is the process of monitoring the status of the project to update the project schedule and managing changes to the schedule baseline.

C. Is concerned mainly with activities that are on the critical path.

D. Should focus primarily on activities that are difficult to carry out.

Project Cost Management
(Section 7 of the *PMBOK® Guide*)

101. Project Cost Management includes all of the following processes EXCEPT:

A. Plan cost management.

B. Level resources.

C. Determine budget.

D. Control costs.

102. The cost management plan has all of the following characteristics EXCEPT:

A. It is based on project cost estimates and is separate from the project management plan.

B. It may specify variance thresholds for monitoring cost performance to indicate an agreed-upon amount of variation to be allowed before some action needs to be taken.

C. It may specify the level of precision, which is the degree to which activity cost estimates will be rounded up or down.

D. It describes how the project costs will be planned, structured, and controlled.

103. All of the following are true about cost estimates EXCEPT:

A. Cost estimates are generally expressed in units of some currency (i.e., dollars, euros, yen, etc.), although in some instances other units of measure, such as staff hours or staff days, are used to facilitate comparisons by eliminating the effects of currency fluctuations.

B. Costs are estimated for all resources that will be charged to the project.

C. Information in the risk register should not be considered in cost estimates, because risks can be either threats or opportunities and their impacts tend to balance out.

D. A cost estimate is a quantitative assessment of the likely costs for resources required to complete the activity. Cost estimates may be presented at the activity level or in summary form.

104. An activity cost estimate includes all of the following resource categories EXCEPT:

A. Labor.

B. Materials.

C. Equipment.

D. Time shortages.

105. Parametric estimating involves:

A. Defining cost or duration parameters of the project life cycle.

B. Calculating individual cost estimates for each work package and integrating them to obtain the total cost of the project.

C. Using a statistical relationship between relevant historical data and other variables to calculate a cost estimate for project work.

D. Using the actual cost of a previous similar project to estimate the cost of the current project.

106. Analogous cost estimating:

A. Integrates bottom-up estimating techniques with relevant statistical relationships to estimate the cost of the current project.

B. Relies on the actual cost of previous, similar projects as the basis for estimating the cost of the current project.

C. Is used most frequently in the later phases of a project.

D. Summarizes estimates for individual work packages to estimate the cost of the current project.

107. Which of the following represents processes concerned with establishing and controlling the cost baseline?

A. Plan Resource Management and Control Costs.

B. Estimate Costs, Develop Budget, and Adhere to Baseline.

C. Determine Budget and Control Costs.

D. Plan Resource Management, Cost Estimating, and Cost Control.

108. The cost baseline has all of the following characteristics EXCEPT:

A. It is the approved version of the time-phased project budget, excluding any management reserves, and is used as a basis for comparison with actual results.

B. It shows the actual cost expenditures throughout the project life cycle.

C. It is developed as a summation of the approved budgets for the different schedule activities.

D. It is typically displayed in the form of an S-curve.

109. Project cost control includes all of the following EXCEPT:

A. Informing appropriate stakeholders of all approved changes and associated costs.

B. Monitoring cost performance to isolate and understand variances from the approved cost baseline.

C. Influencing the factors that create changes to the authorized cost baseline.

D. Allocating the overall estimates to individual work packages to establish a cost baseline.

110. **You have been promoted to the position of project manager for a large project, due to the abrupt transfer of the previous project manager. On the first day in your new, exciting position, you find a folder on your desk entitled: Earned Value Management. In that folder, you find only the following chart related to your project with the Data Date of a few days ago:**

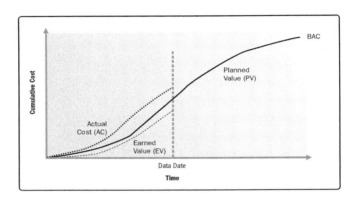

Based on this chart, you conclude that:

A. The project is below budget and probably ahead of schedule.

B. The project is over budget and probably behind schedule.

C. The project is below budget but probably behind schedule.

D. The performance on this project compared to budget and schedule cannot be determined because this chart does not show any values.

Cumulative data for questions 111–116:

BAC = 200

PV = 100

AC = 120

EV = 80

111. Assuming that all future work will be performed at the budgeted rate, the estimate at completion (EAC) is:

    A. 200.

    B. 220.

    C. 240.

    D. 260.

112. Assuming that what the project has experienced to date can be expected to continue in the future, the estimate at completion (EAC) is:

    A. 300.

    B. 325.

    C. 350.

    D. 375.

113. Assuming that future work will be performed at an efficiency rate that considers both the cost and schedule performance indices because project schedule is a factor that impacts future effort, the estimate at completion (EAC) is:

A. 250.

B. 300.

C. 350.

D. 345.

114. Assuming that what the project has experienced to date can be expected to continue in the future, the variance at completion (VAC) is:

A. −80.

B. −100.

C. +100.

D. +200.

115. Assuming that all future work will be performed at the budgeted rate, the estimate to complete (ETC) is:

A. 120.

B. 140.

C. 180.

D. 200.

116. Your sponsor specifies that there is no additional money in the budget for your project and asks you to complete the project at the original budget at completion (BAC). To achieve that goal, you and your team must complete the remaining work at the to-complete performance index (TCPI) of:

A. 0.67.

B. 1.00.

C. 1.50.

D. 2.00.

117. The estimate at completion (EAC) is typically based on:

A. The actual costs incurred for work completed (AC), and the estimate to complete (ETC) the remaining work.

B. The actual costs incurred for work completed (AC) and the cumulative cost performance index (CPI).

C. The earned value (EV) and the actual cost for work completed (AC).

D. The cost performance index (CPI) and the cost variance (CV).

118. Your earned value management analysis indicates that your project is falling behind its baseline schedule. You know this because the cumulative EV is much:

A. Higher than the cumulative AC.

B. Higher than the cumulative PV.

C. Lower than the cumulative PV.

D. Lower than the cumulative CPI.

119. Which of the following cumulative measures indicates that your project is about 9% under budget?

    A. The cumulative AC was 100, and the cumulative EV was 110.

    B. The cumulative PV was 100, and the cumulative AC was 110.

    C. The cumulative AC was 110, and the cumulative EV was 100.

    D. The cumulative EV was 100, and the cumulative PV was 110.

120. Earned value management (EVM) is a commonly used:

    A. Analysis of the value of the equipment that has been installed in the project as of the status date.

    B. Analysis of the sum of the labor costs that have been incurred on the project to date.

    C. Method of performance measurement for projects.

    D. Method of measuring the amount of money that has been spent on the project to date.

121. **During the sixth monthly update on a 10-month, $300,000 project, analysis of the earned value management data shows that the cumulative PV is $190,000, the cumulative AC is $120,000, and the cumulative EV is $150,000. In planning its action, the project management team can conclude all of the following from these measures EXCEPT:**

A. Less has been accomplished than was planned.

B. Less has been spent than was planned.

C. Continuing performance at the same efficiency with no management intervention, the project will probably be completed behind schedule and under budget.

D. Continuing performance at the same efficiency with no management intervention, the project will probably be completed ahead of schedule and over budget.

122. **In earned value management, the cost variance is equal to:**

A. EV minus PV.

B. EV minus AC.

C. AC minus EV.

D. PV minus EV.

123. Earned value (EV) involves all of the following EXCEPT:

A. Value of the work performed expressed in terms of the budget authorized for that work.

B. Actual cost for an activity or work breakdown structure (WBS) component.

C. Progress measurement criteria, which should be established for each WBS component to measure work in progress.

D. Budget associated with the authorized work that has been completed.

124. If cumulative PV = 100, cumulative EV = 98, and cumulative AC = 104, the project is likely to be:

A. Ahead of schedule.

B. Headed for a cost overrun.

C. Operating at project cost projections.

D. Under budget at completion.

Cumulative data for questions 125–126:

Item	PV	AC	EV
1	10,000	11,000	10,000
2	9,000	8,000	7,000
3	8,000	8,000	8,000
4	7,000	7,000	5,000

125. Which item is MOST over budget?

A. Item 1.

B. Item 2.

C. Item 3.

D. Item 4.

126. Which item has the LOWEST SPI?

A. Item 1.

B. Item 2.

C. Item 3.

D. Item 4.

Project Quality Management

(Section 8 of the *PMBOK® Guide*)

127. Project Quality Management includes the processes for incorporating the organization's quality policy regarding planning, managing, and controlling project and product quality requirements in order to:

A. Meet stakeholders' objectives.

B. Improve process capability.

C. Control products, services, and results.

D. Meet standards of performance for the project team.

128. Quality and grade are not the same. A fundamental distinction is that:

A. Quality as a delivered performance or result is the degree to which a set of inherent characteristics fulfills requirements; grade as a design intent is a category assigned to deliverables having the same functional use but different technical characteristics.

B. A quality level that fails to meet quality requirements may not be a problem; a low grade of quality is always a problem.

C. Delivering the required levels of quality is not included in the responsibilities of the project manager and the project team.

D. Delivering the required levels of grade is not included in the responsibilities of the project manager and the project team.

129. Understanding, evaluating, defining, and managing requirements are essential to satisfying:

A. Customer expectations.

B. The scope statement.

C. Upper management.

D. Functional requirements.

130. All of the following are primary benefits of meeting quality requirements EXCEPT:

A. Less rework.

B. Higher productivity.

C. Lower costs.

D. Fewer change orders.

131. Inputs to control quality include all of the following EXCEPT:

A. Project management plan.

B. Quality metrics.

C. Work performance data.

D. PERT chart.

132. The quality management plan is a component of the _____, which describes how the organization's quality policies will be implemented.

    A. Project management plan

    B. Program management plan

    C. Project scope

    D. Governance management plan

133. Manage quality is the process of:

    A. Applying planned, systematic quality activities to ensure effective policing and conformance of the project team to the approved specifications.

    B. Providing the project team and stakeholders with standards by which project performance is measured.

    C. Translating the quality management plan into executable quality activities that incorporate the organization's quality policies into the project.

    D. Assuring the implementation of appropriate specifications, which generally reduces the probability of the project being completed on schedule.

134. Cost of quality includes all of the following EXCEPT:

A. Preventing nonconformance to requirements.

B. Appraising the product or service for conformance to requirements.

C. Failing to meet requirements (rework).

D. Operating computers required for the project.

135. Because of the temporary nature of projects and the potential benefits that may be derived from reducing the post-project cost of quality, _____ may choose to invest in product quality improvement, especially in the areas of prevention and appraisal:

A. Sponsoring organizations

B. The project management team

C. The project executive management team

D. The project quality function deployment (QFD) organization

136. **Control charts have all of the following characteristics EXCEPT:**

A. They are used to determine whether or not a process is stable or has predictable performance.

B. They can be used to monitor various types of output variables.

C. They are used to illustrate how various factors might be linked to potential problems or effects.

D. They are graphical displays of process data over time and against established control limits, which has a centerline that assists in detecting a trend of plotted values toward either control limit.

137. **In relation to control charts, what are the upper and lower specification limits based on?**

A. The requirements, reflecting the maximum and minimum values allowed.

B. The control limits.

C. The specifications, reflecting the maximum and minimum values allowed.

D. The requirements and control limits.

138. _____ is the process of auditing the quality requirements and the results from quality control measurements to ensure that appropriate quality standards and operational definitions are used.

A. Plan quality management

B. Manage quality

C. Control quality

D. Plan quality assurance

139. In using cost-benefit analysis in the Plan Quality Management process, it can be noted that:

A. The primary benefit of meeting quality requirements is the reduced cost associated with project quality management activities.

B. The primary benefits of meeting quality requirements include less rework, higher productivity, lower costs, increased stakeholder satisfaction, and increased profitability.

C. The primary cost of meeting quality requirements is the increased rework to ensure stakeholder satisfaction.

D. Quality cost cannot be evaluated in relationship to the expected benefit of quality in a given project.

140. Benchmarking involves comparing actual or planned project practices to those of comparable projects with all of the following characteristics EXCEPT:

A. To identify best practices and generate ideas for improvement.

B. To provide a basis for measuring performance.

C. Within the performing organization or outside of it.

D. Within the same application area but not in a different application area.

141. The basis for continuous quality improvement is the:

A. Plan-do-check-act (PDCA) cycle as defined by Shewhart and modified by Deming.

B. Process decision program chart (PDPC).

C. Ready-aim-fire (RAF) cycle linked by results.

D. Conceptualize-design-execute-finish (CDEF) cycle.

142. All of the following are true about affinity diagrams EXCEPT:

A. They are used to identify the key issues and the suitable alternatives to be prioritized as a set of decisions for implementation.

B. They are similar to mind-mapping techniques.

C. They are used to generate ideas that can be linked to form organized patterns of thought about a problem.

D. They can be used in project management to give structure to the decomposition of scope and enhance the creation of the WBS.

143. All of the following are considerations for tailoring in Project Quality Management EXCEPT:

A. Standards are regulatory compliance.

B. Policy compliance and auditing.

C. Continuous improvement.

D. Stakeholder management.

144. Planning quality management to identify quality requirements and/or standards for the project and its deliverables and documenting how the project will demonstrate compliance with quality requirements is part of the:

A. Conceptual phase.

B. Planning Process Group.

C. Project implementation phase.

D. Control Quality process.

Project Resource Management
(Section 9 of the *PMBOK® Guide*)

145. The major processes of Project Resource Management are:

A. Leadership, Management, Team Building, and Negotiation.

B. Develop Project Staffing Plan, Recruit Project Team, Administer Personnel Actions, and Manage Labor Relations.

C. Plan Organizational Structure, Build Project Team, Develop Communications Plan, and Manage Team Conflicts.

D. Plan Resource Management, Estimate Activity Resources, Acquire Resources, Develop Team, Manage Team, and Control Resources.

146. The Responsibility Assignment Matrix (RAM) is:

A. Used for development of the project budget and network diagrams.

B. Developed at the activity level and used to closely link project roles and responsibilities to project network activities.

C. Used to illustrate the connections between work packages or activities and project team members. It ensures that there is only one person accountable for any one task to avoid confusion of responsibility.

D. Used to identify accountabilities and responsibilities in individual performance appraisals of project team members.

147. Plan Resource Management should generally include all of the following EXCEPT:

    A. Roles and responsibilities.

    B. Identification of resources.

    C. Acquiring resources.

    D. Project interfaces.

148. Questions that arise when planning the acquisition of team members generally include all of the following EXCEPT:

    A. Whether the resources come from within the organization or from external, contracted sources.

    B. The costs associated with each level of expertise needed for the project.

    C. The compensation of senior executives.

    D. The level of assistance that the organization's human resource department and functional managers are able to provide to the project management team.

149. Acquire resources is the process of confirming resource availability and obtaining the team necessary to complete project activities. The enterprise environmental factors that can influence this process generally include all of the following EXCEPT:

A. Organizational structure.

B. Political philosophy.

C. Competency levels, prior experience, and cost rate.

D. Personnel administration policies, such as those that affect outsourcing.

150. It is important that the resource management plan addresses how team members will be released when they are no longer needed on the project for all of the following reasons EXCEPT:

A. To reduce project costs.

B. To improve morale when smooth transitions to upcoming projects are already planned.

C. To optimize the utilization of human and material resources.

D. To help mitigate resource risks that may occur during or at the end of a project.

151. **To be effective, recognition and rewards systems should have the following characteristics EXCEPT:**

A. Clear criteria for rewards and a planned system for their use to help promote and reinforce desired behaviors.

B. Being based on activities and performance under a person's control.

C. Cultural differences should be considered when determining recognition and rewards.

D. The required performance for rewards should be made unachievable for most team members, to ensure that all team members strive for excellence throughout the project.

152. **Tools and techniques to acquire resources include all of the following EXCEPT:**

A. Decision making.

B. Acquisition.

C. Interpersonal and team skills.

D. Pre-assignment.

153. All of the following are true about conflict management EXCEPT:

A. It is inevitable in a project environment and should be addressed early.

B. It should usually be addressed in private.

C. It should be addressed only when it becomes disruptive, and at an official team meeting.

D. It should be addressed using a direct, collaborative approach.

154. Team building has all of the following characteristics EXCEPT:

A. Team-building activities can vary from a five-minute agenda item in a status review meeting to an off-site, professionally facilitated experience designed to improve interpersonal relationships.

B. Team building should be primarily considered after major conflicts within the project team, because they generally waste precious resource time and cause schedule delays.

C. Team-building strategies are particularly valuable when team members operate from remote locations without the benefit of face-to-face contact.

D. Team building is essential during the front end of a project and is an ongoing process. To effectively manage inevitable changes in the project environment, a continued or renewed team-building effort is required.

155. Training has all of the following characteristics EXCEPT:

  A. It includes all activities designed to enhance the competencies of the project team members.

  B. It can be formal or informal. Examples of training methods include classroom, online, computer-based, on-the-job training from another project team member, mentoring, and coaching.

  C. If project team members lack necessary management or technical skills, the project should be deemed outside the core competencies of the performing organization, outsourced, or abandoned.

  D. If project team members lack the necessary management or technical skills, such skills can be developed as part of the project work.

156. Effective team development strategies and activities are expected to increase the team's performance, which increases the likelihood of meeting project objectives. The evaluation of a team's effectiveness may include all of the following indicators EXCEPT:

  A. Improvements in skills that allow individuals to perform assignments more effectively.

  B. Improvements in competencies that help the team perform better as a unit.

  C. Improvements in the overall project performance as a result of increased intensity of conflict among project team members.

  D. Reduced staff turnover rate.

157. Generally acknowledged techniques for resolving conflict include:

A. Smooth, compromise, collaborate, and co-locating.

B. Accept, compromise, attack, and separate.

C. Accommodate, compromise, force, and collaborate.

D. Withdraw, force, elaborate, and provide sensitivity training.

158. Managing and leading the project team includes:

A. The process of tracking team member performance, providing feedback, resolving issues, and optimizing project performance.

B. Subscribing to the code of professional conduct, but does not involve ensuring that all team members follow professional and ethical behaviors.

C. Influencing the project team to achieve the triple constraints of the project. However, professional and ethical behaviors of project team members are outside the domain of the project management team.

D. Instructing the project team to avoid being caught in repetitive violations of the norms of professional and ethical behaviors specified by the performing organization.

159. Team development stages include:

A. Starting, Organizing, Preparing, Executing, and Closing.

B. Forming, Storming, Norming, Performing, and Adjourning.

C. Acquiring, Managing, Leading, Decision Making, and Releasing.

D. Initiating, Planning, Executing, Monitoring and Controlling, and Closing.

160. All of the following choices represent inputs to the Estimate Activity Resources process EXCEPT:

A. Activity list.

B. Enterprise environmental factors.

C. The deliverable-oriented WBS of a previous, similar project.

D. Resource management plan.

161. Outputs from the Estimate Activity Resources process include:

A. Job descriptions of resources required for the project.

B. Salary schedules for various project resources.

C. Identification of the types and quantities of resources required for each activity in a work package.

D. Analogous estimates of resource requirements for each work package and each work period.

162. Team building has all of the following characteristics EXCEPT:

A. It is the process of helping a group of individuals to build a collaborative and cooperative working environment.

B. It requires handling project team problems decisively and removing the individual(s) responsible for these problems from the team promptly to ensure a productive, smooth project environment.

C. It can help individual team members work together effectively.

D. It can be particularly valuable when team members operate from remote locations without the benefit of face-to-face contact.

163. Motivating involves creating an environment to meet project objectives while providing satisfaction related to what people value most. All of the following are reasons of motivation EXCEPT:

A. Encouraging someone to act.

B. Participating in decision making.

C. Providing accurate criticism in the annual performance review or after the project is completed.

D. Encouraging people to work independently.

Project Communications Management
(Section 10 of the *PMBOK® Guide*)

164. The major processes of Project Communications Management are:

A. Plan Communications Management, Manage Communications, and Monitor Communications.

B. Plan Communications Management, Develop Responses, Report Progress, and Distribute Information.

C. Plan Communications, Distribute Information, and Schedule Reporting.

D. Distribute Information, Report Changes, Update Project Documents, and Accept Project Deliverables.

165. Inputs to the Plan Communications Management process include:

A. Project management plan, project documents, enterprise environmental factors, and organizational process assets.

B. Stakeholder requirements, project scope statement, project budget, and project schedule.

C. Organizational structure, stakeholder analysis, project management plan, and communications barriers.

D. Stakeholder management strategy, RAM, WBS, and administrative procedures.

166. The communications management plan usually contains all of the following EXCEPT:

A. Information to be communicated, including language, format, content, and level of detail.

B. Time frame and frequency for the distribution of required information and receipt of acknowledgment or response, if applicable.

C. Methods or technologies used to convey the information, such as memos, email, and/or press releases.

D. Email archives, correspondence, reports, and documents related to the project from all stakeholders.

167. Hard-copy document management, electronic communications management, and web interfaces to scheduling and project management software are examples of:

A. Project management information systems (PMIS).

B. Internal communications systems (ICS).

C. Internal management systems (IMS).

D. Project records databases.

168. Factors that can affect the choice of communication technology generally include all of the following EXCEPT:

A. Urgency of the need for information.

B. Availability of technology.

C. Executive requirements.

D. Sensitivity and confidentiality of the information.

169. As part of the communications model, the sender is responsible for:

A. Ensuring that the receiver agrees with the message.

B. Confirming that the communication is correctly understood.

C. Presenting the information in the most favorable manner.

D. Decoding the medium correctly.

170. **As part of the communications model, the receiver is responsible for:**

    A. Agreeing with the sender's message.

    B. Pretending that the message is received only partially, to encourage further discussions.

    C. Ensuring that the information is received in its entirety, understood correctly, and acknowledged or responded to appropriately.

    D. Specifying that a verbal message does not give insight to problem areas, and requiring that the message be reduced to writing to avoid potential confusion.

171. **Sources of information typically used to identify and define project communication requirements include all of the following EXCEPT:**

    A. Project organization and stakeholder responsibility relationships.

    B. Disciplines, departments, and specialties involved in the project.

    C. Logistics of how many persons will be involved with the project and at which locations.

    D. Availability of the project sponsor at the project location.

172. Communication activities have many potential dimensions that generally include all of the following EXCEPT:

A. Written, oral, and nonverbal.

B. Internal and external.

C. Conceptual and definitive.

D. Formal and informal.

173. All of the following are information management and distribution tools EXCEPT:

A. Hard-copy document management.

B. Electronic communications management.

C. Inputting project performance data into a spreadsheet or database.

D. Electronic project management tools.

174. Techniques and considerations for effective communications management generally include all of the following EXCEPT:

A. Meeting management techniques, such as preparing an agenda and dealing with conflicts.

B. Conflict management for building consensus and overcoming obstacles.

C. Listening techniques, such as listening actively and removal of barriers that adversely affect comprehension.

D. Providing a more comfortable environment in project conference rooms to strengthen project team cohesion.

175. Monitor Communications is the process of:

A. Ensuring that information is provided on a need-to-know basis only to avoid unnecessary confusion and possible conflicts.

B. Ensuring that the information needs of the project stakeholders are met throughout the entire project life cycle.

C. Providing all project information to all project stakeholders to enhance full buy-in regarding project requirements.

D. Securing and guarding any negative information related to project performance throughout the entire project life cycle to ensure that the project team can continue working on the project with minimal disruption.

Project Risk Management
(Section 11 of the *PMBOK® Guide*)

176. The key processes of Project Risk Management are:

A. Plan Risk Management, Identify Risks, Assess Risks, Mitigate Risks, Transfer Risks, and Document Outcomes.

B. Identify Risks, Plan Risk Management, Evaluate Risks, Develop Risk Responses, Mitigate Risks, and Document Results.

C. Identify Risks, Perform Qualitative Risk Validation, Perform Quantitative Impact Assessment, Develop Risk Response Strategies, Document Response Strategies, and Monitor Risk Responses.

D. Plan Risk Management, Identify Risks, Perform Qualitative Risk Analysis, Perform Quantitative Risk Analysis, Plan Risk Responses, Implement Risk Responses, and Monitor Risks.

177. Strategies typically used to deal with threats or risks that may have negative impacts on project objectives if they occur include all of the following EXCEPT:

A. Interpreting.

B. Avoiding.

C. Transferring.

D. Mitigating.

178. Risk transference nearly always involves:

A. Eliminating risk through beta testing.

B. Policies and procedures for a response system.

C. Accepting a lower profit if some activities overrun their budget.

D. Payment of a risk premium to the party taking on the risk.

179. In the Plan Risk Responses process, an accept strategy for a negative risk or threat indicates that the project team has decided:

A. To agree with the project manager.

B. To eliminate a specific risk or threat, to reduce the probability and/or impact of an adverse risk event to be within acceptable threshold limits, or to pursue an opportunity actively.

C. Not to change the project management plan to deal with a risk, or it is unable to identify any other suitable response strategy.

D. To purchase insurance, or to require performance bonds, warranties, and guarantees.

180. The primary output of the Identify Risks process is the:

A. Risk register.

B. Expected monetary value of the risk events.

C. List of corrective actions.

D. Risk mitigation plan.

181. A thorough analysis of the _____ will help identify potential risks to the project.

A. Risk identification checklist based on historical information and knowledge

B. Project's change control system

C. Project's mission statement

D. Project's schedule and budget

182. All of the following are inputs to the Identify Risks process EXCEPT:

A. Risk management plan.

B. Scope baseline.

C. Risk mitigation plan.

D. Quality management plan.

183. **Outputs from the Plan Risk Responses process include all of the following EXCEPT:**

A. Change requests.

B. Corrective actions.

C. Project documents updates.

D. Project management plan updates.

184. **Tools and techniques of the Perform Quantitative Risk Analysis process include:**

A. Contracting, contingency planning, alternative strategies, and insurance.

B. Interviewing, historical results, workarounds, and response development.

C. Checklists, damage control reports, standard allowances, and inspection.

D. Expert judgment, data gathering, simulations, and decision tree analysis.

185. **As an output of the Perform Quantitative Risk Analysis process, the risk register is updated. These updates generally include:**

   A. Prioritized list of quantified risks.

   B. Qualitative analysis of the threats to ignore and opportunities to accept.

   C. Checklists, corrective actions, and qualified decision trees.

   D. Direction, resources, and contingency costs.

186. **A risk impact assessment to investigate the potential effect on a project objective such as schedule, cost, quality, or performance has the following characteristics EXCEPT:**

   A. Evaluation of each risk can be conducted using a probability and impact matrix that leads to rating the risks as low, moderate, or high priority.

   B. Approaches used in evaluating risk impacts related to project objectives could be relative, numerical, or nonlinear.

   C. Usually, risk-rating rules are specified by the organization in advance of the project and can be tailored to the specific project.

   D. The impact on project objectives should be assessed primarily at the end of the project, as part of the lessons learned.

187. The outputs from the Monitor Risks process include all of the following EXCEPT:

A. Project documents updates.

B. Work breakdown structure (WBS).

C. Change requests.

D. Project management plan updates.

188. The risk rating:

A. Is calculated by multiplying the probability of the occurrence of a risk times its impact (numerical scale) on an objective (e.g., cost, time, scope, or quality) if it were to occur.

B. Is the sum of squares of the scale values assigned to the estimates of probability and impact.

C. Cannot be used to determine whether a risk is considered low, moderate, or high.

D. Is a commonly used technique for risk avoidance.

189. Which one of the following choices is the BEST description of sensitivity analysis?

A. It examines the extent to which the uncertainty of project objectives affects each project element simultaneously.

B. It examines the extent to which the uncertainty of each project element affects the objective being studied when all other uncertain elements are held at their baseline values.

C. It is a method for assessing stakeholders' tolerance to risk.

D. It cannot be used to determine which risks have the most potential impact on the project.

190. All of the following are characteristics of a decision tree EXCEPT:

A. A decision tree is a diagramming and calculation technique for evaluating the implications of a chain of multiple options in the presence of uncertainty.

B. Decision tree analysis is a risk analysis tool that can be used to choose the most appropriate responses.

C. A decision tree is primarily a graphical, qualitative risk analysis technique and is not generally used in quantitative risk analysis.

D. Decision tree analysis uses the expected monetary value (EMV) analysis to calculate the average outcome when the future includes scenarios that may or may not happen.

191. The risk management plan generally includes all of the following EXCEPT:

A. Methodology.

B. Risk strategy.

C. Responses to individual risks.

D. Risk categories.

192. The Perform Qualitative Risk Analysis process assesses the priority of identified risks using all of the following EXCEPT:

A. Relative probability or likelihood of occurrence of identified risks.

B. Impact on project objectives if the identified risks occur.

C. A mathematical technique, such as the expected monetary value (EMV), to create the impression of precision and accuracy.

D. The organization's risk tolerance associated with the project constraints of cost, schedule, scope, and quality.

193. As an output of the Monitor Risks process, an updated risk register generally includes some or all of the following EXCEPT:

A. The work breakdown structure (WBS).

B. Outcomes of risk reassessments, risk audits, and periodic risk reviews.

C. Identification of new risks, updates to probability, impact, priority, response plans, ownership, and other elements of the risk register.

D. Actual outcomes of the project's risks and of the risk responses.

194. SWOT analysis has all of the following characteristics EXCEPT:

A. It is a technique that examines the project from each of the strengths, weaknesses, opportunities, and threats (SWOT) perspectives to increase the breadth of identified risks by including internally generated risks.

B. It identifies strengths and weaknesses of the organization, regardless of the specific project or the general business area.

C. It identifies any opportunities for the project that arise from organizational strengths, and any threats arising from organizational weaknesses.

D. It examines the degree to which organizational strengths offset threats, as well as identifies opportunities that may serve to overcome weaknesses.

195. **All of the following are inputs to the Implement Risk Response process EXCEPT:**

A. Project documents.

B. Project risk management plan.

C. Organizational project assets.

D. Expert judgment.

Project Procurement Management
(Section 12 of the *PMBOK® Guide*)

196. All of the following are inputs to the Plan Procurement Management process EXCEPT:

A. Risk register.

B. Stakeholder register.

C. Procurement strategy.

D. Enterprise environmental factors.

197. Generally, a bid differs from a proposal in that the term:

A. *Bid* is used when the seller selection decision will be based on price.

B. *Bid* is used when technical capability or technical approach are paramount.

C. *Proposal* is used when the selection decision will be based on price.

D. *Proposal* is used when the project time frame is limited.

198. The buyer structures procurement documents, which include all of the following EXCEPT:

A. Procurement statement of work.

B. Bid documents.

C. Source selection criteria and independent cost estimates.

D. Control procurement documents.

199. Approved change requests can generally include all of the following EXCEPT:

A. Modifications to the terms and conditions of the contract.

B. Modification to pricing.

C. Seller invoices.

D. Modification to descriptions of the products, services, or results to be provided.

200. Which of the following is FALSE about advertising as one of the tools and techniques of the Conduct Procurements process?

A. Some government jurisdictions require public advertising of certain types of procurement items.

B. Advertisements in general circulation publications and using online resources can cause public pressure, resulting in bid disputes.

C. Advertising can often be used to expand existing lists of potential sellers.

D. Advertisements can be placed in general circulation publications such as selected newspapers or in specialty trade publications.

201. The buyer, usually through its authorized procurement administrator, provides the seller with _____ as an output of the Control Procurement process.

A. Formal written notice that the contract has been completed

B. Letters of commendation to all project team members

C. Informal notice of acceptance of the deliverables

D. A copy of the internal notice of completion provided to senior management

202. In which type of contracts do buyers need to precisely specify the product or services being procured?

A. Cost plus award fee contracts.

B. Fixed-price contracts.

C. Cost-reimbursable contracts.

D. Partnership contracts.

203. Which of the following is one of the terms used to describe contested changes and potential constructive changes where the buyer and seller cannot reach an agreement on compensation for the change or cannot agree that a change has occurred?

A. Forcing.

B. Mediation.

C. Complaints.

D. Claims.

204. Constructive changes are:

A. Postponed as long as possible to protect the budget.

B. Viewed as negative, quantified, and tabulated.

C. Uniquely identified and documented by project correspondence.

D. Submitted for bids to the relevant vendor list.

205. All legal contractual relationships generally fall into one of the following broad categories EXCEPT:

A. Request for proposal (RFP).

B. Fixed-price contracts.

C. Cost-reimbursable contracts.

D. Time and material contracts (T&M).

206. All of the following are true about the statement of work (SOW) for a procurement EXCEPT:

A. It describes the procurement item in sufficient detail to allow prospective sellers to determine if they are capable of providing the products, services, or results.

B. It should be as ambiguous, incomplete, and wordy as possible to allow for future negotiations.

C. It can include specifications, quantity desired, quality levels, performance data, period of performance, work location, and other requirements.

D. It can be revised and refined as required as it moves through the procurement process until incorporated into a signed agreement.

207. Source selection criteria are developed and used to rate or score seller proposals. These criteria generally have all of the following characteristics EXCEPT:

A. They are often included as a part of the procurement documents.

B. They can be objective or subjective.

C. They may be limited to only the purchase price if the procurement item is readily available from a number of acceptable sellers.

D. They generally require specification of the name of the transportation organization responsible for delivery of procured products.

208. All of the following are tools and techniques of the Conduct Procurements process EXCEPT:

A. Interpersonal and team skills.

B. Bidder conferences.

C. Expert judgment.

D. Source selection analysis.

209. **Cost plus fixed-fee contracts (CPFF) have all of the following characteristics EXCEPT:**

A. Seller is reimbursed for all allowable costs for performing the contract work.

B. Seller receives a fixed-fee payment calculated as a percentage of the actual project costs.

C. Seller receives a fixed-fee payment calculated as a percentage of the initial estimated project costs.

D. The fee is paid only for completed work and does not change due to seller performance unless the project scope changes.

210. **This type of analysis results in a decision as to whether particular work can best be accomplished by the project team or needs to be purchased from outside sources:**

A. Source-selection analysis.

B. Regulations analysis.

C. Make-or-buy analysis.

D. Data-gathering analysis.

211. In many projects, negotiation is:

A. Primarily the concern of contract administration.

B. A discussion aimed at reaching an agreement.

C. A direct result of ineffective decision making.

D. Conducted by senior executives to increase the probability of project success.

Project Stakeholder Management
(Section 13 of the *PMBOK® Guide*)

212. Stakeholders are:

A. The project engineers who design and construct the project.

B. The people, groups, or organizations that could impact or be impacted by a decision, activity, or outcome of the project.

C. The organization's corporate attorneys.

D. The individuals or agencies that control contingency funds and their disbursement through the project management office (PMO).

213. Which of the following is NOT a process in Project Stakeholder Management?

A. Identify Stakeholders.

B. Control Stakeholder Engagement.

C. Monitor Stakeholder Engagement.

D. Manage Stakeholder Engagement.

214. To increase the chances of achieving project success, the project manager should do all of the following EXCEPT:

A. Identify the stakeholders early in the project or phase.

B. Analyze the stakeholders' levels of interest and individual expectations as well as their importance and influence.

C. As much as possible, create conflicts among various stakeholders to allow the project team to get optimal work done.

D. Communicate and work with stakeholders to meet their needs/expectations.

215. You are developing management strategies to effectively engage stakeholders throughout the project life cycle, based on the analysis of their needs, interests, and potential impact on project success. This is known as:

A. Manage Stakeholder Engagement.

B. Monitor Stakeholder Engagement.

C. Plan Stakeholder Engagement.

D. Plan Stakeholder Management.

216. You are involved in the process of communicating and working with stakeholders to meet their needs/expectations, address issues as they occur, and foster appropriate stakeholder engagement in project activities throughout the project life cycle. This is known as:

A. Manage Stakeholder Engagement.

B. Monitor Stakeholder Engagement.

C. Plan Stakeholder Management.

D. Plan Stakeholder Engagement.

217. You are monitoring overall project stakeholder relationships and adjusting strategies and plans for engaging stakeholders. This is known as:

A. Manage Stakeholder Engagement.

B. Plan Stakeholder Engagement.

C. Stakeholders' Relationship Engagement.

D. Monitor Stakeholder Engagement.

218. You are using a classification model for stakeholders' analysis that groups the stakeholders based on their level of authority and their level or concern regarding the project outcomes. This is known as:

A. Power/influence grid.

B. Influence/impact grid.

C. Power/interest grid.

D. Salience model.

219. In developing a stakeholder register, you need to include all of the following EXCEPT:

A. Identification information.

B. Assessment information.

C. Stakeholder classification.

D. Project risk information.

220. Classification of the engagement levels of stakeholders includes all of the following EXCEPT:

A. Resistant.

B. Neutral.

C. Supportive.

D. Manipulative.

221. Manage Stakeholder Engagement involves all of the following activities EXCEPT:

A. Clarifying and resolving issues that have been identified.

B. Avoiding potential concerns that have not yet become issues.

C. Anticipating future problems that may be raised by stakeholders.

D. Managing stakeholders' expectations through negotiation and communication.

222. All of the following statements about Manage Stakeholder Engagement are true EXCEPT:

A. Managing stakeholder engagement helps increase the probability of project success.

B. The ability of stakeholders to influence the project is typically highest during the initial stages and gets progressively lower as the project progresses.

C. The ability of stakeholders to influence the project is typically lowest during the initial stages and gets progressively higher as the project progresses.

D. The project manager is responsible for engaging and managing the various stakeholders in a project and may call upon the project sponsor to assist as needed.

223. Monitor Stakeholder Engagement tools and techniques include all of the following EXCEPT:

A. Decision making.

B. Stakeholder analysis.

C. Meetings.

D. Issue log.

224. The power/interest grid classification model for stakeholders' analysis suggests:

A. Keeping high-power/high-interest stakeholders informed.

B. Keeping high-power/low-interest stakeholders satisfied.

C. Monitoring low-power/high-interest stakeholders.

D. Managing low-power/low-interest stakeholders closely.

225. **During a public hearing regarding your company's proposed state-of-the-art water tower, a highly interested resident of the area challenges you: "Would you have this thing built in your own backyard?" Your best answer can begin by saying:**

A. Given that you are not listed in the stakeholders' register, I cannot take your concerns seriously.

B. I am sorry that you appear to dislike having this water tower as your neighbor. We will look for another location for it.

C. Given that the experts provided ample information that the proposed location is the most suitable, I would be pleased to have this state-of-the-art water tower as a neighbor.

D. If you want to have usable water pressure in your residence, you should not interfere with our work.

226. **Examples of interpersonal skills that a project manager uses most often include all of the following indicators EXCEPT:**

A. Leadership.

B. Influencing.

C. Governance.

D. Effective decision making.

Appendix X3
(Agile, Iterative, Adaptive, and Hybrid Project Environments)

227. The project life cycle is best defined as:

    A. The continuum of a project life cycle.

    B. The phases that a product or service passes through from its start to its completion.

    C. The series of phases that a project passes through from its start to completion.

    D. The various ways requirements and plans are brought from a project charter to completion.

228. Projects following more of the adaptive side of the project life cycle most closely follow the pattern of:

    A. Sequential, iteration-based phases and continuous overlapping phases.

    B. Sequential, iteration-based phases and sequential nonoverlapping phases.

    C. Continuous overlapping phases and agile-based phases.

    D. Agile-based phases and sequential, iteration-based phases.

229. All of the following are Process Groups in adaptive environments EXCEPT:

A. Planning Process Group.

B. Monitoring and Controlling Process Group.

C. Scope Management Process Group.

D. Closing Process Group.

230. Iterative, agile, and adaptive approaches track, review, and regulate progress and performance by maintaining:

A. A detailed to-do list.

B. A backlog.

C. A work breakdown structure.

D. Work packages.

231. _____ life cycles develop a set of high-level plans for the initial requirements and progressively elaborate requirements to an appropriate level of detail for the planning cycle.

A. Predictive

B. Adaptive

C. Plan-driven

D. Program

Appendix X4

232. Project Integration Management includes all of the following EXCEPT:

A. Prevention is preferred over inspection. It is better to design quality into deliverables, rather than to find quality issues during inspection. The cost of preventing mistakes is generally much less than the cost of correcting mistakes when they are found by inspection or during usage.

B. Projects and project management are integrative by nature, with most tasks involving more than one Knowledge Area.

C. The relationships of processes within and between the Project Management Process Groups are iterative.

D. Managing project performance and changes to the project activities.

233. Project Scope Management includes all of the following EXCEPT:

A. Scope can refer to product scope (the features and functions that characterize a product, service, or result), or to project scope (the work performed to deliver a product, service, or result with the specified features and functions).

B. Projects and project management are integrative by nature, with most tasks involving more than one Knowledge Area.

C. Project life cycles range along a continuum from predictive to adaptive or agile. In a life cycle that uses a predictive approach, the project deliverables are defined at the beginning of the project and any changes to the scope are progressively managed. In an adaptive or agile approach, the deliverables are developed over multiple iterations where a detailed scope is defined and approved for each iteration when it begins.

D. Completion of the project scope is measured against the project management plan. Completion of the product scope is measured against the product requirements.

234. Project Schedule Management includes all of the following EXCEPT:

A. Project scheduling provides a detailed plan that represents how and when the project will deliver the products, services, and results defined in the project scope.

B. The project schedule is used as a tool for communication, managing stakeholder expectations, and a basis for performance reporting.

C. Project managers may need to be familiar with sampling, including attribute sampling (the result either conforms or does not conform) and variable sampling (the result is rated on a continuous scale that measures the degree of conformity).

D. When possible, the detailed project schedule should remain flexible throughout the project to adjust for knowledge gained, increased understanding of the risk, and value-added activities.

235. Project Cost Management includes all of the following EXCEPT:

A. Project Cost Management is primarily concerned with the cost of the resources needed to complete project activities, but it should also consider the effect of project decisions on the subsequent recurring cost of using, maintaining, and supporting project deliverables.

B. Different stakeholders will measure project costs in different ways and at different times. Stakeholder requirements for managing costs should be considered explicitly.

C. Predicting and analyzing the prospective financial performance of the project's product may be performed outside the project, or it may be part of Project Cost Management.

D. Measuring and monitoring progress and taking appropriate action.

236. Project Quality Management includes all of the following EXCEPT:

A. Project life cycles range along a continuum from predictive to adaptive or agile. In a life cycle that uses a predictive approach, the project deliverables are defined at the beginning of the project and any changes to the scope are progressively managed. In an adaptive or agile approach, the deliverables are developed over multiple iterations where a detailed scope is defined and approved for each iteration when it begins.

B. Quality and grade are different concepts. Quality is "the degree to which a set of inherent characteristics fulfills requirements" (ISO 9000). Grade is a category assigned to deliverables having the same functional use but with different technical characteristics. The project manager and team are responsible for managing trade-offs associated with delivering the required levels of both quality and grade.

C. Prevention is preferred over inspection. It is better to design quality into deliverables, rather than to find quality issues during inspection. The cost of preventing mistakes is generally much less than the cost of correcting mistakes when they are found by inspection or during usage.

D. Project managers may need to be familiar with sampling, including attribute sampling (the result either conforms or does not conform) and variable sampling (the result is rated on a continuous scale that measures the degree of conformity).

237. Project Resource Management includes all of the following EXCEPT:

A. The project manager is responsible for proactively developing team skills and competences while retaining and improving team satisfaction and motivation.

B. Effort is required to prevent misunderstandings and miscommunication, and the methods, messengers, and messages should be carefully selected.

C. The project manager should be both the leader and the manager of the project team, and should invest suitable effort in acquiring, managing, motivating, and empowering team members.

D. The project manager should be aware of team influences such as the team environment, geographical location of team members, communication among stakeholders, organizational change management, internal and external politics, cultural issues, and organizational uniqueness.

238. Project Communications Management includes all of the following EXCEPT:

A. Communication activities include internal and external, formal and informal, written and oral.

B. Communication can be directed upward to senior management stakeholders, downward to team members, or horizontally to peers. This will affect the format and content of the message.

C. Physical resource management is concentrated on allocating and utilizing the physical resources needed for successful completion of the project in an efficient and effective way. Failure to manage and control resources efficiently may reduce the chance of completing the project successfully.

D. Effective communication creates a bridge between diverse stakeholders whose differences will generally have an impact or influence upon the project execution or outcome, so it is vital that all communication is clear and concise.

239. Project Risk Management includes all of the following EXCEPT:

A. All projects are risky. Organizations choose to take project risk in order to create value, while balancing risk and reward.

B. Project Risk Management aims to identify and manage risks that are not covered by other project management processes.

C. Risk exists at two levels within every project: Individual project risk is an uncertain event or condition that, if it occurs, has a positive or negative effect on one or more project objectives. Overall project risk is the effect of uncertainty on the project as a whole, arising from all sources of uncertainty, including individual risks, representing the exposure of stakeholders to the implications of variations in project outcome, both positive and negative. Project Risk Management processes address both levels of risk in projects.

D. Ignoring overall project risk to focus on specific project risks, because that will take care of project overall risk.

240. **Project Procurement Management includes all of the following EXCEPT:**

A. All projects are risky. Organizations choose to take project risk in order to create value, while balancing risk and reward.

B. Procurement involves agreements that describe the relationship between a buyer and a seller. Agreements can be simple or complex, and the procurement approach should reflect the degree of complexity. An agreement can be a contract, a service-level agreement, an understanding, a memorandum of agreement, or a purchase order.

C. Agreements must comply with local, national, and international laws regarding contracts.

D. The project manager should ensure that all procurements meet the specific needs of the project, while working with procurement specialists to ensure that organizational policies are followed.

241. Project Stakeholder Management includes all of the following EXCEPT:

A. The process of identifying and engaging stakeholders for the benefit of the project is iterative, and should be reviewed and updated routinely, particularly when the project moves into a new phase or if there are significant changes in the organization or the wider stakeholder community.

B. Physical resource management is concentrated on allocating and utilizing the physical resources needed for successful completion of the project in an efficient and effective way. Failure to manage and control resources efficiently may reduce the chances of completing the project successfully.

C. The key to effective stakeholder engagement is a focus on continuous communication with all stakeholders. Stakeholder satisfaction should be identified and managed as a key project objective.

D. To increase the chances of success, the process of stakeholder identification and engagement should commence as soon as possible after the project charter has been approved, the project manager has been assigned, and the team begins to form.

Appendix X5

(Summary of Tailoring Considerations for Knowledge Areas)

242. When tailoring processes for Project Schedule Management, you should consider all of these EXCEPT:

    A. Life cycle approach.

    B. Knowledge management.

    C. Project dimensions.

    D. Governance.

243. When tailoring processes for Project Quality Management, you should consider all of these EXCEPT:

    A. Stakeholder engagement.

    B. Policy compliance and auditing.

    C. Project complexity, uncertainty, and product novelty.

    D. Standards and regulatory compliance.

244. **When tailoring processes for Project Resource Management, you should consider all of these EXCEPT:**

A. Diversity.

B. Physical location.

C. Number of team members.

D. Life cycle approach.

245. **When tailoring processes for Project Risk Management, you should consider all of these EXCEPT:**

A. Project complexity.

B. Project importance.

C. Project size.

D. Project duration.

246. **When tailoring processes for Project Stakeholder Management, you should consider all of these EXCEPT:**

A. Complexity of stakeholder relationships.

B. Stakeholder diversity.

C. Complexity technology.

D. Stakeholder engagement.

247. When tailoring processes for Project Cost Management, you should consider all of these EXCEPT:

A. Estimating and budgeting.

B. Earned value management.

C. Governance.

D. Continuous improvement.

Glossary

248. The types and quantities of resources required for each activity in a work package.

A. Resource requirements.

B. Resource breakdown structure.

C. Organizational chart.

D. Resource package.

249. A project life cycle that is iterative or incremental.

A. Waterfall.

B. Adaptive life cycle.

C. Predictive life cycle.

D. Progressive development.

250. Tom, a project manager of a large defense project, is using a technique for estimating the duration of an activity in his project using historical data from a similar activity or project.

A. Bottom-up estimating.

B. Three-point estimating.

C. Analogous estimating.

D. Parametric estimating.

251. **Dawn is a project manager in a successful product launch in Silicon Valley. She often comes across factors in the planning process that are considered to be true, real, or certain, without proof or demonstration. These are called:**

A. Constraints.

B. Dependencies.

C. Leads and lags.

D. Assumptions.

252. **For smaller projects, what is the supporting documentation that could be used to support the details used in establishing project estimates such as assumptions, constraints, level of detail, ranges, and confidence levels?**

A. Basis of estimates.

B. Cost estimates.

C. Duration estimates.

D. Resource estimates.

253. **A documented economic feasibility study used to establish validity of the benefits of a selected component lacking sufficient definition and that is used as a basis for the authorization of further project management activities.**

   A. Business need.

   B. Business case.

   C. Benefits realization.

   D. Case study.

254. **A technique for systematically reviewing materials using a list for accuracy and completeness.**

   A. Constraints analysis.

   B. Assumptions analysis.

   C. Checklist analysis.

   D. Flowchart analysis.

255. **An analytical technique to determine the information needs of the project stakeholders through interviews, workshops, study of lessons learned from previous projects, etc.**

   A. Communication requirements technology.

   B. Project management information system (PMIS).

   C. Information management system (IMS).

   D. Communication requirements analysis.

256. **Time or money allocated in the schedule or cost baseline for known risks with active response strategies.**

    A. Management reserve.

    B. Contingency reserve.

    C. Top-down reserve.

    D. Risk allocation reserve.

257. **All costs incurred over the life of the product by investment in preventing nonconformance to requirements, appraisal of the product or service for conformance to requirements, and failure to meet requirements.**

    A. Budget at completion (BAC).

    B. Cost of errors (COE).

    C. Cost of quality (COQ).

    D. Total cost (TC).

258. **Any activity on the critical path in a project schedule.**

    A. Critical chain activity.

    B. Positive slack activity.

    C. Critical path activity.

    D. Negative slack activity.

259. **The amount of time that a schedule activity can be delayed or extended from its early start date without delaying the project finish date or violating a schedule constraint.**

    A. Free lag.

    B. Free float.

    C. Negative float.

    D. Total float.

260. **An adaptive project life cycle in which the deliverable is produced through a series of iterations that successively add functionality within a predetermined time frame. The deliverable contains the necessary and sufficient capability to be considered complete only after the final iteration.**

    A. Incremental life cycle.

    B. Waterfall life cycle.

    C. Critical path life cycle.

    D. Program life cycle.

261. **An adaptive project life cycle in which the deliverable matures through a series of repeated cycles. The deliverable contains the necessary and sufficient capability to be considered complete at the end of each cycle. Each repeated cycle further enhances the capability of the deliverable.**

   A. Project life cycle.

   B. Iterative life cycle.

   C. Product life cycle.

   D. Business analysis life cycle.

262. **A form of project life cycle in which the project scope, time, and cost are determined in the early phases of the life cycle.**

   A. Program life cycle.

   B. Product life cycle.

   C. Predictive life cycle.

   D. Adaptive life cycle.

263. **The iterative process of increasing the level of detail in a project management plan as greater amounts of information and more accurate estimates become available.**

A. Waterfall schedule.

B. Gantt chart.

C. Summary schedule.

D. Progressive elaboration.

264. **Which of the below represents the BEST definition for quality audits?**

A. A quality audit is a structured, independent process to determine if project activities comply with organizational and project policies, processes, and procedures.

B. A project document that includes quality management issues, recommendations for corrective actions, and a summary of findings from quality control activities, and may include recommendations for process, project, and product improvements.

C. A policy specific to the Project Quality Management Knowledge Area, it establishes the basic principles that should govern the organization's actions as it implements its system for quality management.

D. A description of a project or product attribute and how to measure it.

265. Which of the below represents the BEST definition for a RACI chart?

A. A hierarchical representation of resources by category and type.

B. A common type of responsibility assignment matrix that uses responsible, accountable, consult, and inform statuses to define the involvement of stakeholders in project activities.

C. A calendar that identifies the working days and shifts upon which each specific resource is available.

D. A bar chart showing the amount of time that a resource is scheduled to work over a series of time periods.

266. What is the BEST way to describe the requirements documentation?

A. A grid that links product requirements from their origin to the deliverables that satisfy them.

B. A component of the program or project management plan that describes how requirements will be analyzed, documented, and managed.

C. A description of how individual requirements meet the business need for the project.

D. A condition or capability that is necessary to be present in a product, service, or result to satisfy a business need.

267. What is the BEST definition for residual risk?

A. A risk response strategy whereby the project team decides to acknowledge the risk and not take any action unless the risk occurs.

B. The degree of uncertainty an organization or individual is willing to accept in anticipation of a reward.

C. A risk response strategy whereby the project team acts to eliminate the threat or protect the project from its impact.

D. The risk that remains after risk responses have been implemented.

268. Which of the below represents the BEST definition for resource leveling?

A. A resource optimization technique in which adjustments are made to the project schedule to optimize the allocation of resources and which may affect critical path.

B. The types and quantities of resources required for each activity in a work package.

C. A bar chart showing the amount of time that a resource is scheduled to work over a series of time periods.

D. A hierarchical representation of resources by category and type.

269. **Which definition BEST describes rolling wave planning?**

A. A grid that shows the project resources assigned to each work package.

B. An iterative planning technique in which the work to be accomplished in the near term is planned in detail, while the work in the future is planned at a higher level.

C. A component of the project or program management plan that establishes the criteria and the activities for developing, monitoring, and controlling the schedule.

D. A technique to identify early and late start dates, as well as early and late finish dates, for the uncompleted portions of project activities.

270. **What is the definition of cost baseline?**

A. A financial analysis tool used to determine the benefits provided by a project against its costs.

B. A measure of the cost efficiency of budgeted resources expressed as the ratio of earned value to actual cost.

C. The approved version of the time-phased project budget, excluding any management reserves, which can be changed only through formal change control procedures and is used as a basis for comparison to actual results.

D. The amount of budget deficit or surplus at a given point in time, expressed as the difference between the earned value and the actual cost.

271. What is the BEST description for scope baseline?

A. A component of the program or project management plan that describes how the scope will be defined, developed, monitored, controlled, and validated.

B. The sum of the products, services, and results to be provided as a project.

C. The uncontrolled expansion to product or project scope without adjustments to time, cost, and resources.

D. The approved version of a scope statement, work breakdown structure (WBS), and its associated WBS dictionary, that can be changed using formal change control procedures and is used as a basis for comparison to actual results.

272. Which phrase BEST describes the source selection criteria?

A. A set of attributes desired by the buyer which a seller is required to meet or exceed to be selected for a contract.

B. A technique of systematically gathering and analyzing quantitative and qualitative information to determine whose interests should be taken into account throughout the project.

C. A project document including the identification, assessment, and classification of project stakeholders.

D. A narrative description of products, services, or results to be delivered by the project.

273. How would you define the statement of work (SOW)?

A. The uncontrolled expansion to product or project scope without adjustments to time, cost, and resources.

B. A narrative description of products, services, or results to be delivered by the project.

C. The approved version of a scope statement, work breakdown structure (WBS), and its associated WBS dictionary, that can be changed using formal change control procedures and is used as a basis for comparison to actual results.

D. Formal responses from sellers to a request for proposal or other procurement document specifying the price, commercial terms of sale, and technical specifications or capabilities the seller will do for the requesting organization that, if accepted, would bind the seller to perform the resulting agreement.

274. Which statement below BEST describes Tailoring?

A. Project documents that describe the activities used to determine if the product meets the quality objectives stated in the quality management plan.

B. A component of the resource management plan that describes when and how team members will be acquired and how long they will be needed.

C. Determining the appropriate combination of processes, inputs, tools, techniques, outputs, and life cycle phases to manage a project.

D. A partially complete document in a predefined format that provides a defined structure for collecting, organizing, and presenting information and data.

275. Select the answer that BEST describes test and evaluation documents:

A. Determining the appropriate combination of processes, inputs, tools, techniques, outputs, and life cycle phases to manage a project.

B. A dependent activity that logically comes after another activity in a schedule.

C. A special type of bar chart used in sensitivity analysis for comparing the relative importance of the variables.

D. Project documents that describe the activities used to determine if the product meets the quality objectives stated in the quality management plan.

276. What is a work breakdown structure (WBS)?

A. A hierarchical decomposition of the total scope of work to be carried out by the project team to accomplish the project objectives and create the required deliverables.

B. The approved version of a scope statement, work breakdown structure (WBS), and its associated WBS dictionary, that can be changed using formal change control procedures and is used as a basis for comparison to actual results.

C. The sum of the products, services, and results to be provided as a project.

D. A contract between a service provider (either internal or external) and the end user that defines the level of service expected from the service provider.

277. Which is the BEST definition to describe the work package?

A. The uncontrolled expansion to product or project scope without adjustments to time, cost, and resources.

B. The work defined at the lowest level of the work breakdown structure for which cost and duration are estimated and managed.

C. A component of the project or program management plan that describes how the scope will be defined, developed, monitored, controlled, and validated.

D. The approved version of a scope statement, work breakdown structure (WBS), and its associated WBS dictionary, that can be changed using formal change control procedures and is used as a basis for comparison to actual results.

Q & As

FOR THE
PMBOK® GUIDE
SIXTH EDITION
Answers

Introduction
(Section 1 of the *PMBOK® Guide*)

1. Answer: D.
PMBOK® Guide, page 4, Section 1.2.1

What is a project?
A project is a temporary endeavor undertaken to create a unique product, service, or result.

2. Answer: B.
PMBOK® Guide, page 10, Section 1.2.2

What is project management?
Project management is the application of knowledge, skills, tools, and techniques to project activities to meet the project requirements.

3. Answer: C.

PMBOK® Guide, page 15, Section 1.2.3.3

Portfolio Management
...

Portfolio management refers to the centralized management of one or more portfolios to achieve strategic objectives. Portfolio management focuses on ensuring that projects and programs are reviewed to prioritize resource allocation and that the management of the portfolio is consistent with and aligned to organizational strategies.

4. Answer: C.

PMBOK® Guide, page 34, Section 1.2.6.4

Arguably, all responses are suitable during project planning. However, the three most important questions for defining project success are:
- What does success look like for the project?
- How will success be measured?
- What factors may impact success?

The answer on communication requirements is an important consideration, but it occurs at a more detailed planning level for creating a project communications plan, which leads to project success.

5. Answer: B.

PMBOK® Guide, page 11, Section 1.2.3.1

Program Management
A program is defined as a group of related projects, subsidiary programs, and program activities managed in a coordinated manner to obtain benefits not available from managing them individually. Programs are not large projects.

6. Answer: D.
PMBOK® Guide, pages 11–13, Section 1.2.3.1

Relationship Between Project Management, Operations Management, and Organizational Strategy
Operations management is responsible for overseeing, directing, and controlling business operations. Operations evolve to support the day-to-day business, and are necessary to achieve strategic and tactical goals of the business. Examples include production operations, manufacturing operations, accounting operations, software support, and maintenance.

Though temporary in nature, projects can help achieve the organizational goals when they are aligned with the organization's strategy. Organizations sometimes change their operations, products, or systems by creating strategic business initiatives that are developed and implemented through projects. Projects require project management activities and skill sets, while operations require business process management, operations management activities, and skill sets.

Operations and Project Management
Changes in business operations may be the focus of a dedicated project—especially if there are substantial changes to business operations as a result of a new product or service delivery. Ongoing operations are outside of the scope of a project; however, there are intersecting points where the two areas cross.

Projects can intersect with operations at various points during the product life cycle, such as:
- At each closeout phase;
- When developing a new product, upgrading a product, or expanding outputs;
- While improving operations or the product development process; or
- Until the end of the product life cycle.

At each point, deliverables and knowledge are transferred between the project and operations for implementation of the delivered work. This implementation occurs through a transfer of project resources to operations toward the end of the project, or through a transfer of operational resources to the project at the start.

Operations are ongoing endeavors that produce repetitive outputs, with resources assigned to do basically the same set of tasks according to the standards institutionalized in a product life cycle. Unlike the ongoing nature of operations, projects are temporary endeavors.

7. Answer: D.
PMBOK® Guide, page 15, Section 1.2.3.3

...

Portfolio management aligns components (projects, programs, or operations) to the organizational strategy, organized into portfolios or subsidiary portfolios to optimize project or program objectives, dependencies, costs, timelines, benefits, resources, and risks. This allows organizations to have an overall view of how the strategic goals are reflected in the portfolio, institute appropriate governance management, and authorize human, financial, or material resources to be allocated based on expected performance and benefits.

8. Answer: C.
PMBOK® Guide, page 2, Section 1.1.1

Project Management Body of Knowledge
The standard (*PMBOK® Guide*) identifies the processes that are considered good practices on most projects, most of the time. The standard also identifies the inputs and outputs that are usually associated with those processes.

9. Answer: B.
PMBOK® Guide, page 19, Section 1.2.4.1

Project Life Cycle
A project life cycle is the series of phases that a project passes through from its start to its completion. It provides the basic framework for managing the project. This basic framework applies regardless of the specific project work involved. The phases may be sequential, iterative, or overlapping. All projects can be mapped to the generic life cycle as shown in Figure 1–5.

10. Answer: D.

PMBOK® Guide, page 19, Section 1.2.4.1

...

Characteristics of the Project Life Cycle

Project life cycles can be predictive or adaptive. Within a project life cycle, there are generally one or more phases that are associated with the development of the product, service, or result. These are called a development life cycle. Development life cycles can be predictive, iterative, incremental, adaptive, or a hybrid model. Explanation here is only provided for predictive and iterative life cycles. Refer to Section 1.2.4.1 for the other development life cycles.

In a predictive life cycle, the project scope, time, and cost are determined in the early phases of the life cycle. Any changes to the scope are carefully managed. Predictive life cycles may also be referred to as waterfall life cycles. In an iterative life cycle, the project scope is generally determined early in the project life cycle, but time and cost estimates are routinely modified as the project team's understanding of the product increases. Iterations develop the product through a series of repeated cycles, while increments successively add to the functionality of the product.

While project cost and staffing levels *can be* steady, for larger and complex projects, costs and staffing levels are subject to change and therefore *not likely* to be steady throughout the project life cycle.

11. Answer: D.

PMBOK® Guide, pages 19–21, Sections 1.2.4.1 and 1.2.4.2

Predictive Life Cycles
Predictive life cycles (also known as fully plan-driven) are ones in which the project scope, and the time and cost required to deliver that scope, are determined as early in the project life cycle as practically possible. These projects proceed through a series of sequential or overlapping phases, with each phase generally focusing on a subset of project activities and project management processes. The work performed in each phase is usually different in nature from that in the preceding and subsequent phases; therefore, the makeup and skills required of the project team may vary from phase to phase.

Iterative and Incremental Life Cycles
Iterative and incremental life cycles are ones in which project phases (also called iterations) intentionally repeat one or more project activities as the project team's understanding of the product increases. Iterations develop the product through a series of repeated cycles, while increments successively add to the functionality of the product. These life cycles develop the product both iteratively and incrementally.

Product life cycle. The series of phases that represent the evolution of a product, from concept through delivery, growth, maturity, and to retirement.

Project life cycle. The series of phases that a project passes through from its initiation to its closure.

12. Answer: B.

PMBOK® Guide, page 19, Section 1.2.4.1

Project life cycles can be predictive or adaptive. Within a project life cycle, there are generally one or more phases that are associated with the development of the product, service, or result. These are called a development life cycle. Development life cycles can be predictive, iterative, incremental, adaptive, or a hybrid model. The explanation here is only provided for predictive, iterative, and adaptive life cycles. Refer to Section 1.2.4.1 for the other development life cycles.

- In a predictive life cycle, the project scope, time, and cost are determined in the early phases of the life cycle. Any changes to the scope are carefully managed. Predictive life cycles may also be referred to as waterfall life cycles.
- In an iterative life cycle, the project scope is generally determined early in the project life cycle, but time and cost estimates are routinely modified as the project team's understanding of the product increases. Iterations develop the product through a series of repeated cycles, while increments successively add to the functionality of the product.
- Adaptive life cycles are agile, iterative, or incremental. The detailed scope is defined and approved before the start of an iteration. Adaptive life cycles are also referred to as agile or change-driven life cycles. Also see Appendix X3.

13. Answer: B.

PMBOK® Guide, page 23, Section 1.2.4.5

Project management processes are grouped into five categories known as Project Management Process Groups (or Process Groups):

- **Initiating Process Group.** Those processes performed to define a new project or a new phase of an existing project by obtaining authorization to start the project or phase.
- **Planning Process Group.** Those processes required to establish the scope of the project, refine the objectives, and define the course of action required to attain the objectives that the project was undertaken to achieve.
- **Executing Process Group.** Those processes performed to complete the work defined in the project management plan to satisfy the project specifications.
- **Monitoring and Controlling Process Group.** Those processes required to track, review, and regulate the progress and performance of the project; identify any areas in which changes to the plan are required; and initiate the corresponding changes.
- **Closing Process Group.** Those processes performed to finalize all activities across all Process Groups to formally close the project or phase.

14. Answer: A.

PMBOK® Guide, page 22, Section 1.2.4.4

Project management processes may contain overlapping activities that occur throughout the project.

15. Answer: C.
PMBOK® Guide, page 23, Section 1.2.4.5

The project management processes are linked by specific inputs and outputs where the result or outcome of one process may become the input to another process that is not necessarily in the same Process Group.

16. Answer: C.
PMBOK® Guide, pages 34–35, Section 1.2.6.4

One of the most common challenges in project management is determining whether or not a project is successful. Traditionally, the project management metrics of time, cost, scope, and quality have been the most important factors in defining the success of a project. More recently, practitioners and scholars have determined that project success should also be measured with consideration toward achievement of the project objectives.

Project stakeholders may have different ideas as to what the successful completion of a project will look like and which factors are the most important. It is critical to clearly document the project objectives and to select objectives that are measurable. Project success may include additional criteria linked to the organizational strategy and to the delivery of business results.

17. Answer: C.
PMBOK® Guide, pages 30–32, Section 1.2.6.1

The project business case is a documented economic feasibility study used to establish the validity of the benefits of a selected component lacking sufficient definition and that is used as a basis for the authorization of further project management activities. The business case lists the objectives and reasons for project initiation. . . .

18. Answer: A.

PMBOK® Guide, page 33, Section 1.2.6.2

The benefits management plan describes key elements of the benefits and may include, but is not limited to, documenting:

- Target benefits (e.g., the expected tangible and intangible value to be gained by the implementation of the project; financial value is expressed as net present value);
- Strategic alignment (e.g., how well the project benefits align to the business strategies of the organization);
- Time frame for realizing benefits (e.g., benefits by phase, short-term, long-term, and ongoing);
- Benefits owner (e.g., the accountable person to monitor, record, and report realized benefits throughout the time frame established in the plan);
- Metrics (e.g., the measures to be used to show benefits realized, direct measures, and indirect measures);
- Assumptions (e.g., factors expected to be in place or to be in evidence); and
- Risks (e.g., risks for realization of benefits).

19. Answer: B.
PMBOK® Guide, page 26, Section 1.2.4.7

Throughout the life cycle of a project, a significant amount of data is collected, analyzed, and transformed. Project data are collected as a result of various processes and are shared within the project team. The collected data are analyzed in context, aggregated, and transformed to become project information during various processes. Information is communicated verbally or stored and distributed in various formats as reports.

Project data are regularly collected and analyzed throughout the project life cycle. The following definitions identify key terminology regarding project data and information:

- **Work performance data.** The raw observations and measurements identified during activities performed to carry out the project work. Examples include reported percent of work physically completed, quality and technical performance measures, start and finish dates of schedule activities, number of change requests, number of defects, actual costs, actual durations, etc. Project data are usually recorded in a Project Management Information System (PMIS) and in project documents.
- **Work performance information.** The performance data collected from various controlling processes, analyzed in context, and integrated based on relationships across areas. Examples of performance information are status of deliverables, implementation status for change requests, and forecast estimates to complete.
- **Work performance reports.** The physical or electronic representation of work performance information compiled in project documents, which is intended to generate decisions or raise issues, actions, or awareness. Examples include status reports, memos, justifications, information notes, electronic dashboards, recommendations, and updates.

Work performance analysis is a required activity, but not a source of project data.

20. Answer: A.

PMBOK® Guide, page 28, Section 1.2.5

Tailoring is necessary because each project is unique; not every process, tool, technique, input, or output identified in the *PMBOK® Guide* is required on every project. Tailoring should address the competing constraints of scope, schedule, cost, resources, quality, and risk. The importance of each constraint is different for each project, and the project manager tailors the approach for managing these constraints based on the project environment, organizational culture, stakeholder needs, and other variables.

In tailoring project management, the project manager should also consider the varying levels of governance that may be required and within which the project will operate, as well as considering the culture of the organization. In addition, consideration of whether the customer of the project is internal or external to the organization may affect project management tailoring decisions.

But since tailoring requires significant project management experience and knowledge, tailoring the project to suit a project manager's skill set is likely to be uncommon.

The Environment in Which Projects Operate

(Section 2 of the *PMBOK® Guide*)

21. Answer: D.

PMBOK® Guide, page 38, Section 2.2.1

Enterprise Environmental Factors

Enterprise environmental factors (EEFs) refer to conditions, not under the control of the project team, that influence, constrain, or direct the project. Enterprise environmental factors are considered inputs to most planning processes, may enhance or constrain project management options, and may have a positive or negative influence on the outcome.

EEFs vary widely in type or nature. These factors need to be considered if the project is to be effective. EEFs include, but are not limited to, the factors below.

The following EEFs are internal to the organization:

- **Organizational culture, structure, and governance.** Examples include vision, mission, values, beliefs, cultural norms, leadership styles, hierarchy and authority relationships, organizational styles, ethics, and codes of conduct.
- **Geographic distribution of facilities and resources.** Examples include factory locations, virtual teams, shared systems, and cloud computing.
- **Infrastructure.** Examples include existing facilities, equipment, organizational telecommunications channels, information technology hardware, availability, and capacity.
- **Information technology software.** Examples include scheduling software tools, configuration management systems, web interfaces to other online automated systems, and work authorization systems.

- **Resource availability.** Examples include contracting and purchasing constraints, approved providers and subcontractors, and collaboration agreements.
- **Employee capability.** Examples include existing human resources expertise, skills, competencies, and specialized knowledge.

The following EEFs are external to the organization:

- **Marketplace conditions.** Examples include competitors, market share brand recognition, and trademarks.
- **Social and cultural influences and issues.** Examples include political climate, codes of conduct, ethics, and perceptions.
- **Legal restrictions.** Examples include country or local laws and regulations related to security, data protection, business conduct, employment, and procurement.
- **Commercial databases.** Examples include benchmarking results, standardized cost estimating data, industry risk study information, and risk databases.
- **Academic research.** Examples include industry studies, publications, and benchmarking results.
- **Government or industry standards.** Examples include regulatory agency regulations and standards related to products, production, environment, quality, and workmanship.
- **Financial considerations.** Examples include currency exchange rates, interest rates, inflation rates, tariffs, and geographic location.

22. Answer: C.

PMBOK® Guide, pages 48–49, Section 2.4.4.3

There are several types of PMO structures in organizations, each varying in the degree of control and influence they have on projects within the organization, such as the following:

- **Supportive.** Supportive PMOs provide a consultative role to projects by supplying templates, best practices, training, access to information, and lessons learned from other projects. This type of PMO serves as a project repository. The degree of control provided by the PMO is low.
- **Controlling.** Controlling PMOs provide support and require compliance through various means. Compliance may involve adopting project management frameworks or methodologies; using specific templates, forms, and tools; or conformance to governance. The degree of control provided by the PMO is moderate.
- **Directive.** Directive PMOs take control of the projects by directly managing the projects. The degree of control provided by the PMO is high.

23. Answer: A.

PMBOK® Guide, page 49, Section 2.4.4.3

Project Management Office

...

A primary function of a PMO is to support project managers in a variety of ways, which may include, but are not limited to:

- Managing shared resources across all projects administered by the PMO;
- Identifying and developing project management methodologies, best practices, and standards;
- Coaching, mentoring, training, and oversight;
- Monitoring compliance with project management standards, policies, procedures, and templates by means of project audits;
- Developing and managing project policies, procedures, templates, and other shared documentation (organizational process assets); and
- Coordinating communication across projects.

PMOs do not generally intervene in a project's direction, especially without communicating with the project manager.

24. Answer: C.
PMBOK® Guide, page 41, Section 2.3.2

Tacit knowledge is personal and difficult to express, and is generally not found in organizational knowledge repositories. One of the important purposes of knowledge management is to transform tacit knowledge into explicit knowledge, which can then be stored in repositories.

The organizational knowledge repositories for storing and retrieving information include, but are not limited to:
- Configuration management knowledge repositories containing the versions of software and hardware components and baselines of all performing organization standards, policies, procedures, and any project documents;
- Financial data repositories containing information such as labor hours, incurred costs, budgets, and any project cost overruns;
- Historical information and lessons learned knowledge repositories (e.g., project records and documents, all project closure information and documentation, information regarding both the results of previous project selection decisions and previous project performance information, and information from risk management activities);
- Issue and defect management data repositories containing issue and defect status, control information, issue and defect resolution, and action item results;
- Data repositories for metrics used to collect and make available measurement data on processes and products; and
- Project files from previous projects (e.g., scope, cost, schedule, and performance measurement baselines, project calendars, project schedule network diagrams, risk registers, risk reports, and stakeholder registers).

25. Answer: B.
PMBOK® Guide, page 39, Section 2.2.2

Enterprise Environmental Factors
Enterprise environmental factors (EEFs) refer to conditions, not under the control of the project team, that influence, constrain, or direct the project. Enterprise environmental factors are considered inputs to most planning processes, may enhance or constrain project management options, and may have a positive or negative influence on the outcome. EEFs vary widely in type or nature. These factors need to be considered if the project is to be effective. EEFs include, but are not limited to, the factors below.

The following EEFs are internal to the organization:
- **Organizational culture, structure, and governance.** Examples include vision, mission, values, beliefs, cultural norms, leadership styles, hierarchy and authority relationships, organizational styles, ethics, and codes of conduct.
- **Geographic distribution of facilities and resources.** Examples include factory locations, virtual teams, shared systems, and cloud computing.
- **Infrastructure.** Examples include existing facilities, equipment, organizational telecommunications channels, information technology hardware, availability, and capacity.
- **Information technology software.** Examples include scheduling software tools, configuration management systems, web interfaces to other online automated systems, and work authorization systems.
- **Resource availability.** Examples include contracting and purchasing constraints, approved providers and subcontractors, and collaboration agreements.
- **Employee capability.** Examples include existing human resources expertise, skills, competencies, and specialized knowledge.

The following EEFs are external to the organization:

- **Marketplace conditions.** Examples include competitors, market share brand recognition, and trademarks.
- **Social and cultural influences and issues.** Examples include political climate, codes of conduct, ethics, and perceptions.
- **Legal restrictions.** Examples include country or local laws and regulations related to security, data protection, business conduct, employment, and procurement.
- **Commercial databases.** Examples include benchmarking results, standardized cost estimating data, industry risk study information, and risk databases.
- **Academic research.** Examples include industry studies, publications, and benchmarking results.
- **Government or industry standards.** Examples include regulatory agency regulations and standards related to products, production, environment, quality, and workmanship.
- **Financial considerations.** Examples include currency exchange rates, interest rates, inflation rates, tariffs, and geographic location.
- **Physical environmental elements.** Examples include working conditions, weather, and constraints.

An organization's value and principle, while not explicitly stated, are related to organizational culture and thus are internal to an organization.

26. Answer: C.

PMBOK® Guide, page 39, Section 2.3

Organizational process assets (OPAs) are the plans, processes, policies, procedures, and knowledge bases specific to and used by the performing organization. They may be grouped into two categories:
- Processes, policies, and procedures; and
- Organizational knowledge bases.

27. Answer: B.

PMBOK® Guide, page 40, Section 2.3.1

The organization's processes and procedures for conducting project work for Initiating and Planning include, but are not limited, to:
- Guidelines and criteria for tailoring the organization's set of standard processes and procedures to satisfy the specific needs of the project;
- Specific organizational standards such as policies (e.g., human resources policies, health and safety policies, security and confidentiality policies, quality policies, procurement policies, and environmental policies);
- Product and project life cycles, and methods and procedures (e.g., project management methods, estimation metrics, process audits, improvement targets, checklists, and standardized process definitions for use in the organization);
- Templates (e.g., project management plans, project documents, project registers, report formats, contract templates, risk categories, risk statement templates, probability and impact definitions, probability and impact matrices, and stakeholder register templates); and
- Preapproved supplier lists and various types of contractual agreements (e.g., fixed-price, cost-reimbursable, and time and material contracts).

Traceability matrices are important considerations during the project execution.

28. Answer: D.

PMBOK® Guide, pages 40–41, Section 2.3.1

The organization's processes and procedures for conducting project work for Executing and Monitoring and Controlling include, but are not limited, to:

- Change control procedures, including the steps by which performing organization standards, policies, plans, and procedures or any project documents will be modified, and how any changes will be approved and validated;
- Traceability matrices;
- Financial controls procedures (e.g., time reporting, required expenditure and disbursement reviews, accounting codes, and standard contract provisions);
- Issue and defect management procedures (e.g., defining issue and defect controls, identifying and resolving issues and defects, and tracking action items);
- Resource availability control and assignment management;
- Organizational communication requirements (e.g., specific communication technology available, authorized communication media, record retention policies, videoconferencing, collaborative tools, and security requirements);
- Procedures for prioritizing, approving, and issuing work authorizations;
- Templates (e.g., risk register, issue log, and change log);
- Standardized guidelines, work instructions, proposal evaluation criteria, and performance measurement criteria; and
- Product, service, or result verification and validation procedures.

Project closing guidelines are included in OPAs for the Closing Process Group.

29. Answer: D.

PMBOK® Guide, page 42, Section 2.4.1

Projects operate within the constraints imposed by the organization through their structure and governance framework. To operate effectively and efficiently, the project manager needs to understand where responsibility, accountability, and authority reside within the organization. This understanding will help the project manager effectively use his or her power, influence, competence, leadership, and political capabilities to successfully complete the project.

The interaction of multiple factors within an individual organization creates a unique system that impacts the project operating in that system. The resulting organizational system determines the power, influence, interests, competence, and political capabilities of the people who are able to act within the system. The system factors include, but are not limited to:
- Management elements,
- Governance frameworks, and
- Organizational structure types.

Project managers should consider tailoring the project management processes based on these system factors.

30. Answer: A.

PMBOK® Guide, page 42, Section 2.4.1

Systems are typically the responsibility of an organization's management. The organization's management examines the optimizational trade-offs between the components and the system in order to take the appropriate action to achieve the best outcomes for the organization. The results of this examination will impact the project under consideration.

31. Answer: C.

PMBOK® Guide, page 43, Section 2.4.2.1

Governance is the framework within which authority is exercised in organizations. This framework includes, but is not limited to:
- Rules,
- Policies,
- Procedures,
- Norms,
- Relationships,
- Systems, and
- Processes.

This framework influences how:
- Objectives of the organization are set and achieved,
- Risk is monitored and assessed, and
- Performance is optimized.

Specific techniques are low-level details not usually specified by governance.

32. Answer: A.

PMBOK® Guide, pages 44–45, Section 2.4.3

Management elements are the components that comprise the key functions or principles of general management in the organization. The general management elements are allocated within the organization according to its governance framework and the organizational structure type selected.

The Role of the Project Manager
(Section 3 of the *PMBOK® Guide*)

33. Answer: D.
PMBOK® Guide, page 60, Section 3.4.4

Leadership Skills
Leadership skills involve the ability to guide, motivate, and direct a team. These skills may include demonstrating essential capabilities such as negotiation, resilience, communication, problem solving, critical thinking, and interpersonal skills. Projects are becoming increasingly more complicated with more and more businesses executing their strategy through projects. Project management is more than just working with numbers, templates, charts, graphs, and computing systems. A common denominator in all projects is people. People can be counted, but they are not numbers.

34. Answer: A.

PMBOK® Guide, page 54, Section 3.3.2

The Project

The ability to communicate with stakeholders, including the team and sponsors, applies across multiple aspects of the project including, but not limited to:

- Developing finely tuned skills using multiple methods (e.g., verbal, written, and nonverbal);
- Creating, maintaining, and adhering to communications plans and schedules;
- Communicating predictably and consistently;
- Seeking to understand the project stakeholders' communication needs (communication may be the only deliverable that some stakeholders receive until the project's end product or service is completed);
- Making communications concise, clear, complete, simple, relevant, and tailored;
- Including important positive and negative news;
- Incorporating feedback channels; and
- Relationship skills involving the development of extensive networks of people throughout the project manager's spheres of influence. These networks include formal networks such as organizational reporting structures. However, the informal networks that project managers develop, maintain, and nurture are more important. Informal networks include the use of established relationships with individuals such as subject matter experts and influential leaders. Use of these formal and informal networks allows the project manager to engage multiple people in solving problems and navigating the bureaucracies encountered in a project.

35. Answer: C.
PMBOK® Guide, page 66, Section 3.4.5.2

Personality
Personality refers to the individual differences in characteristic patterns of thinking, feeling, and behaving. Personality characteristics or traits include, but are not limited to:
...
- Cultural (e.g., measure of sensitivity to other cultures, including values, norms, and beliefs); and
- Emotional (e.g., ability to perceive emotions and the information they present and to manage them; measure of interpersonal skills).

36. Answer: A.
PMBOK® Guide, page 66, Section 3.5

The role of the project manager is twofold when performing integration on the project:
- Project managers play a key role in working with the project sponsor to understand the strategic objectives and ensure the alignment of the project objectives and results with those of the portfolio, program, and business areas. In this way, project managers contribute to the integration and execution of the strategy; and
- Project managers are responsible for guiding the team to work together to focus on what is really essential at the project level. This is achieved through the integration of processes, knowledge, and people.

37. Answer: C.
PMBOK® Guide, pages 66–67, Sections 3.5, 3.5.1, 3.5.2, 3.5.3

Integration is a critical skill for project managers. Integration takes place at three different levels: process, cognitive, and context.

Performing Integration at the Process Level
Project management may be seen as a set of processes and activities that are undertaken to achieve the project objectives. Some of these processes may take place once (e.g., the initial creation of the project charter), but many others overlap and occur several times throughout the project. Although there is no stated definition on how to integrate the project processes, it is clear that a project has a small chance of meeting its objective when the project manager fails to integrate the project processes where they interact.

Integration at the Cognitive Level
There are many different ways to manage a project, and the method selected typically depends on the specific characteristics of the project, including its size, how complicated the project or organization may be, and the culture of the performing organization. It is clear that the personal skills and abilities of the project manager are closely related to the way in which the project is managed.

The project manager should strive to become proficient in all of the Project Management Knowledge Areas. In concert with proficiency in these Knowledge Areas, the project manager applies experience, insight, leadership, and technical and business management skills to the project. Finally, it is the project manager's ability to integrate the processes in these Knowledge Areas that makes it possible to achieve the desired project results.

Integration at the Context Level

There have been many changes in the context in which business and projects take place today compared to a few decades ago. New technologies have been introduced. Social networks, multicultural aspects, virtual teams, and new values are part of the new reality of projects. An example is knowledge and people integration in the context of a large, cross-functional project implementation involving multiple organizations. The project manager considers the implications of this context in communications planning and knowledge management for guiding the project team.

38. Answer: D.

PMBOK® Guide, page 68, Section 3.5

Complexity within projects is a result of the organization's system behavior, human behavior, and the uncertainty at work in the organization or its environment. The three dimensions of complexity are defined as follows:

- **System behavior.** The interdependencies of components and systems.
- **Human behavior.** The interplay between diverse individuals and groups.
- **Ambiguity.** Uncertainty of emerging issues and lack of understanding or confusion.

39. Answer: D.

PMBOK® Guide, page 51, Section 3.1

The project manager plays a critical role in the leadership of a project team in order to achieve the project's objectives. This role is clearly visible throughout the project. Many project managers become involved in a project from its initiation through closing. However, in some organizations, a project manager may be involved in evaluation and analysis activities prior to project initiation. These activities may include consulting with executive and business unit leaders on ideas for advancing strategic objectives, improving organizational performance, or meeting customer needs. In some organizational settings, the project manager may also be called upon to manage or assist in business analysis, business case development, and aspects of portfolio management for a project. A project manager may also be involved in follow-on activities related to realizing business benefits from the project. The role of a project manager may vary from organization to organization. Ultimately, the project management role is tailored to fit the organization in the same way that the project management processes are tailored to fit the project.

Because project managers are generally responsible for "temporary" endeavors, they are least likely to be involved in ensuring efficient operations, at least in their role as a project manager.

40. Answer: A.

PMBOK® Guide, pages 52–53, Section 3.3.1

Project managers fulfill numerous roles within their sphere of influence. These roles reflect the project manager's capabilities and are representative of the value and contributions of the project management profession. Figure 3-1 illustrates some examples of the project manager's sphere of influence.

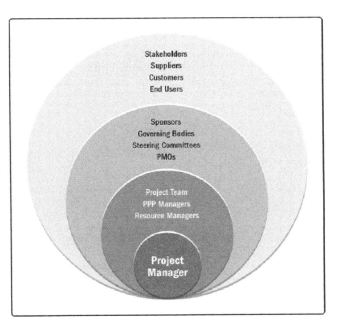

41. Answer: B.

PMBOK® Guide, page 56, Section 3.4.1

Recent PMI studies applied the *Project Manager Competency Development (PMCD) Framework* – Third Edition to the skills needed by project managers through the use of the PMI Talent Triangle®. The Talent Triangle focuses on three key skill sets:

- **Technical project management skills.** The knowledge, skills, and behaviors related to specific domains of project, program, and portfolio management; the technical aspects of performing one's role.
- **Leadership capabilites.** The knowledge, skills, and behaviors needed to guide, motivate, and direct a team, to help an organization achieve its business goals.
- **Strategic and business management expertise.** The knowledge of and expertise in the industry and organization that enhance performance and better deliver business outcomes.

42. Answer: D.

PMBOK® Guide, page 64, Section 3.4.5, Table 3-1

The words *leadership* and *management* are often used interchangeably. However, they are not synonymous. The word *management* is more closely associated with directing another person to get from one point to another using a known set of expected behaviors. In contrast, leadership involves working with others through discussion or debate in order to guide them from one point to another.

The method that a project manager chooses to employ reveals a distinct difference in behavior, self-perception, and project role. Table 3-1 compares management and leadership on several important levels.

Project managers need to employ both leadership and management in order to be successful. The skill is in finding the right balance for each situation. The way in which management and leadership are employed often shows up in the project manager's leadership style.

43. Answer: B.

PMBOK® Guide, pages 62–63, Section 3.4.4.3

B is the best answer because it is the most comprehensive response. A and C are not the best responses because they are not as comprehensive as B (plus, cultural is not listed in the section even though it can be a source of soft power). D is correct, but not as comprehensive as B.

Various forms of power listed in Section 3.4.4.3 include, but are not limited to:

- Positional (sometimes called formal, authoritative, legitimate) (e.g., formal position granted in the organization or team);
- Informational (e.g., control of gathering or distribution);
- Referent (e.g., respect or admiration that others hold for the individual, credibility gained);
- Situational (e.g., gained due to unique situation such as a specific crisis);
- Personal or charismatic (e.g., charm, attraction);
- Relational (e.g., participates in networking, connections, and alliances);
- Expert (e.g., skill, information possessed; experience, training, education, certification);
- Reward-oriented (e.g., ability to give praise, monetary or other desired items);
- Punitive or coercive (e.g., ability to invoke discipline or negative consequences);
- Ingratiating (e.g., application of flattery or other common ground to win favor or cooperation);
- Pressure-based (e.g., limit freedom of choice or movement for the purpose of gaining compliance to desired action);
- Guilt-based (e.g., imposition of obligation or sense of duty);
- Persuasive (e.g., ability to provide arguments that move people to a desired course of action); and
- Avoiding (e.g., refusing to participate).

44. **Answer: D.**

PMBOK® Guide, page 66, Section 3.4.5.2

Personality refers to the individual differences in characteristic patterns of thinking, feeling, and behaving. Personality characteristics or traits include, but are not limited to:

- Authentic (e.g., accepts others for what and who they are, shows open concern);
- Courteous (e.g., ability to apply appropriate behavior and etiquette);
- Creative (e.g., ability to think abstractly, to see things differently, to innovate);
- Cultural (e.g., measure of sensitivity to other cultures, including values, norms, and beliefs);
- Emotional (e.g., ability to perceive emotions and the information they present and to manage them; measure of interpersonal skills);
- Intellectual (e.g., measure of human intelligence over multiple aptitudes);
- Managerial (e.g., measure of management practice and potential);
- Political (e.g., measure of political intelligence and making things happen);
- Service-oriented (e.g., evidence of willingness to serve other people);
- Social (e.g., ability to understand and manage people); and
- Systemic (e.g., drive to understand and build systems).

An effective project manager will have some level of ability with each of these characteristics in order to be successful. Each project, organization, and situation requires that the project manager emphasize different aspects of personality.

45. Answer: B.

PMBOK® Guide, page 65, Section 3.4.5.1

Project managers may lead their teams in many ways. The style a project manager selects may be a personal preference, or the result of the combination of multiple factors associated with the project.

Some of the most common examples of these styles include, but are not limited to:

- Laissez-faire (e.g., allowing the team to make their own decisions and establish their own goals; also referred to as taking a hands-off style);
- Transactional (e.g., focus on goals, feedback, and accomplishment to determine rewards; management by exception);
- Servant leader (e.g., demonstrates commitment to serve and put other people first; focuses on other people's growth, learning, development, autonomy, and well-being; concentrates on relationships, community, and collaboration; leadership is secondary and emerges after service);
- Transformational (e.g., empowering followers through idealized attributes and behaviors, inspirational motivation, encouragement for innovation and creativity, and individual consideration);
- Charismatic (e.g., able to inspire; is high-energy, enthusiastic, self-confident; holds strong convictions); and
- Interactional (e.g., a combination of transactional, transformational, and charismatic).

46. Answer: B.

PMBOK® Guide, page 68, Section 3.5.4

Complexity as a characteristic or property of a project is typically defined as:
- Containing multiple parts,
- Possessing a number of connections among the parts,
- Exhibiting dynamic interactions among the parts, and
- Exhibiting behavior produced as a result of those interactions that cannot be explained as the simple sum of the parts (e.g., emergent behavior).

47. Answer: D.

PMBOK® Guide, pages 51–52, Section 3.1

Project managers and conductors are similar, with regard to managing the membership and roles, responsibilities for their teams, and proper knowledge and skills. However, unlike conductors who should possess musical knowledge and understanding of all instructors, project managers may not have the similar level of knowledge of all activities on projects. Project managers should possess project management knowledge, technical knowledge, understanding, and experience of the overall project to be effective managers.

Project Integration Management
(Section 4 of the *PMBOK® Guide*)

48. Answer: A.
PMBOK® Guide, page 70, Introduction; and page 71, Figure 4-1

Project Integration Management
The Project Integration Management processes are as follows:

4.1 Develop Project Charter—The process of developing a document that formally authorizes the existence of a project and provides the project manager with the authority to apply organizational resources to project activities.

4.2 Develop Project Management Plan—The process of defining, preparing, and coordinating all plan components and consolidating them into an integrated project management plan.

4.3 Direct and Manage Project Work—The process of leading and performing the work defined in the project management plan and implementing approved changes to achieve the project's objectives.

4.4 Manage Project Knowledge—The process of using existing knowledge and creating new knowledge to achieve the project's objectives and contribute to organizational learning.

4.5 Monitor and Control Project Work—The process of tracking, reviewing, and reporting overall progress to meet the performance objectives defined in the project management plan.

4.6 Perform Integrated Change Control—The process of reviewing all change requests; approving changes and managing changes to deliverables, organizational process assets, project documents, and the project management plan; and communicating the decisions.

4.7 Close Project or Phase—The process of finalizing all activities for the project, phase, or contract.

Figure 4-1 provides an overview of the Project Integration Management processes. The Project Integration Management processes are presented as discrete processes with defined interfaces while, in practice, they overlap and interact in ways that cannot be completely detailed in the *PMBOK® Guide*.

49. Answer: C.

PMBOK® Guide, pages 75–77, Section 4.1

Develop Project Charter

Develop Project Charter is the process of developing a document that formally authorizes the existence of a project and provides the project manager with the authority to apply organizational resources to project activities. The key benefits of this process are that it provides a direct link between the project and the strategic objectives of the organization, creates a formal record of the project, and shows the organizational commitment to the project. This process is performed once or at predefined points in the project.

The project charter establishes a partnership between the performing and requesting organizations. In the case of external projects, a formal contract is typically the preferred way to establish an agreement. A project charter may still be used to establish internal agreements within an organization to ensure proper delivery under the contract. The approved project charter formally initiates the project. A project manager is identified and assigned as early in the project as is feasible, preferably while the project charter is being developed and always prior to the start of planning. The project charter can be developed by the sponsor or the project manager in collaboration with the initiating entity. This collaboration allows the project manager to have a better understanding of the project purpose, objectives, and expected benefits. This understanding will better allow for efficient resource allocation to project activities. The project charter provides the project manager with the authority to plan, execute, and control the project.

Projects are initiated by an entity external to the project such as a sponsor, program or project management office (PMO), or a portfolio governing body chairperson or authorized representative. The project initiator or sponsor should be at a level that is appropriate to procure funding and commit resources to the project. Projects are initiated due to internal business needs or external influences. These needs or influences often trigger the creation of a needs analysis, feasibility study, business case, or description of the situation that the project will address. Chartering a project validates alignment of the project to the strategy and ongoing work of the organization. A project charter is not considered to be a contract because there is no consideration or money promised or exchanged in its creation.

50. Answer: D.
PMBOK® Guide, page 95, Section 4.3.2.2

Project Management Information System (PMIS)
The PMIS provides access to information technology (IT) software tools, such as scheduling software tools, work authorization systems, configuration management systems, information collection and distribution systems, as well as interfaces to other online automated systems such as corporate knowledge base repositories. Automated gathering and reporting on key performance indicators (KPIs) can be part of this system.

51. **Answer: D.**

PMBOK® Guide, page 118, Section 4.6.2.1; and page 120, Section 4.6.2.5

Perform Integrated Change Control: Tools and Techniques

Expert Judgment

Expertise should be considered from individuals or groups with specialized knowledge of or training in the following topics:

- Technical knowledge of the industry and focus area of the project,
- Legislation and regulations,
- Legal and procurement,
- Configuration management, and
- Risk management.

Meetings

Change control meetings are held with a change control board (CCB) that is responsible for meeting and reviewing the change requests and approving, rejecting, or deferring change requests. Most changes will have some sort of impact on time, cost, resources, or risks. Assessing the impact of the changes is an essential part of the meeting. Alternatives to the requested changes may also be discussed and proposed. Finally, the decision is communicated to the request owner or group.

The CCB may also review configuration management activities. The roles and responsibilities of these boards are clearly defined and agreed upon by the appropriate stakeholders and are documented in the change management plan. CCB decisions are documented and communicated to the stakeholders for information and follow-up actions.

52. Answer: A.

PMBOK® Guide, pages 113 and 115, Section 4.6

Perform Integrated Change Control

Perform Integrated Change Control is the process of reviewing all change requests; approving changes and managing changes to deliverables, project documents, and the project management plan; and communicating the decisions. This process reviews all requests for changes to project documents, deliverables, or the project management plan and determines the resolution of the change requests. The key benefit of this process is that it allows for documented changes within the project to be considered in an integrated manner while addressing overall project risk, which often arises from changes made without consideration of the overall project objectives or plans. This process is performed throughout the project.

The Perform Integrated Change Control process is conducted from project start through completion and is the ultimate responsibility of the project manager. Change requests can impact the project scope and the product scope, as well as any project management plan component or any project document. Changes may be requested by any stakeholder involved with the project and may occur at any time throughout the project life cycle. The applied level of change control is dependent upon the application area, complexity of the specific project, contract requirements, and the context and environment in which the project is performed.

Before the baselines are established, changes are not required to be formally controlled by the Perform Integrated Change Control process. Once the project is baselined, change requests go through this process. As a general rule, each project's configuration management plan should define which project artifacts need to be placed under configuration control. Any change in a configuration element should be formally controlled and will require a change request.

Although changes may be initiated verbally, they should be recorded in written form and entered into the change management and/or configuration management system. Change requests may require information on estimated schedule impacts and estimated cost impacts prior to approval. Whenever a change request may impact any of the project baselines, a formal integrated change control process is always required. Every documented change request needs to be either approved, deferred, or rejected by a responsible individual, usually the project sponsor or project manager. The responsible individual will be identified in the project management plan or by organizational procedures. When required, the Perform Integrated Change Control process includes a change control board (CCB), which is a formally chartered group responsible for reviewing, evaluating, approving, deferring, or rejecting changes to the project and for recording and communicating such decisions.

Approved change requests can require new or revised cost estimates, activity sequences, schedule dates, resource requirements, and/or analysis of risk response alternatives. These changes can require adjustments to the project management plan and other project documents. Customer or sponsor approval may be required for certain change requests after CCB approval, unless they are part of the CCB.

53. Answer: B.

PMBOK® Guide, page 118, Section 4.6.2.2

Change Control Tools

Configuration control is focused on the specification of both the deliverables and the processes, while change control is focused on identifying, documenting, and approving or rejecting changes to the project documents, deliverables, or baselines.

54. Answer: C.

PMBOK® Guide, page 115, Section 4.6; and Glossary

Every documented change request needs to be either approved, deferred, or rejected by a responsible individual, usually the project sponsor or project manager. The responsible individual will be identified in the project management plan or by organizational procedures. When required, the Perform Integrated Change Control process includes a change control board (CCB), which is a formally chartered group responsible for reviewing, evaluating, approving, deferring, or rejecting changes to the project and for recording and communicating such decisions.

Approved change requests can require new or revised cost estimates, activity sequences, schedule dates, resource requirements, and/or analysis of risk response alternatives. These changes can require adjustments to the project management plan and other project documents. Customer or sponsor approval may be required for certain change requests after CCB approval, unless they are part of the CCB.

Change control board (CCB). A formally chartered group responsible for reviewing, evaluating, approving, delaying, or rejecting changes to the project, and for recording and communicating such decisions.

55. **Answer: B.**
PMBOK® Guide, pages 118–119, Section 4.6.2.2

Change Control Tools
Tool selection should be based on the needs of the project stakeholders, including organizational and environmental considerations and/or constraints. Tools should support the following configuration management activities:

- **Identify configuration item.** Identification and selection of a configuration item to provide the basis for which the product configuration is defined and verified, products and documents are labeled, changes are managed, and accountability is maintained.
- **Record and report configuration item status.** Information recording and reporting about each configuration item.
- **Perform configuration item verification and audit.** Configuration verification and configuration audits ensure that the composition of a project's configuration items is correct and that corresponding changes are registered, assessed, approved, tracked, and correctly implemented. This ensures that the functional requirements defined in the configuration documentation are met.

Tools should support the following change management activities as well:

- **Identify changes.** Identifying and selecting a change item for processes or project documents.
- **Document changes.** Documenting the change into a proper change request.
- **Decide on changes.** Reviewing the changes; approving, rejecting, deferring, or making any other decision about changes to the project documents, deliverables, or baselines.
- **Track changes.** Verifying that the changes are registered, assessed, approved, and tracked and communicating final results to stakeholders.

Tools are also used to manage the change requests and the resulting decisions. Additional considerations should be made for communications to assist the change control board (CCB) members in their duties, as well as to distribute the decisions to the appropriate stakeholders.

56. Answer: A.
PMBOK® Guide, pages 121 and 123, Section 4.7

Close Project or Phase
Close Project or Phase is the process of finalizing
all activities for the project, phase, or contract. The
key benefits of this process are: the project or phase
information is archived, the planned work is completed,
and organizational team resources are released to pursue
new endeavors. This process is performed once or at
predefined points in the project.

When closing the project, the project manager reviews the
project management plan to ensure that all project work
is completed and that the project has met its objectives.
The activities necessary for the administrative closure of
the project or phase include, but are not limited to:
- Actions and activities necessary to satisfy completion
  or exit criteria for the phase or project such as:
  o Making certain that all documents and
    deliverables are up to date and that all issues are
    resolved;
  o Confirming the delivery and formal acceptance of
    deliverables by the customer;
  o Ensuring that all costs are charged to the project;
  o Closing project accounts;
  o Reassigning personnel;
  o Dealing with excess project material;
  o Reallocating project facilities, equipment, and
    other resources; and
  o Elaborating the final project reports as required by
    organizational policies.
- Activities related to the completion of the contractual
  agreements applicable to the project or project phase
  such as:
  o Confirming the formal acceptance of the seller's
    work,
  o Finalizing open claims,
  o Updating records to reflect final results, and
  o Archiving such information for future use.

- Activities needed to:
  - Collect project or phase records,
  - Audit project success or failure,
  - Manage knowledge sharing and transfer,
  - Identify lessons learned, and
  - Archive project information for future use by the organization.
- Actions and activities necessary to transfer the project's products, services, or results to the next phase or to production and/or operations.
- Collecting any suggestions for improving or updating the policies and procedures of the organization, and sending them to the appropriate organizational unit.
- Measuring stakeholder satisfaction.

The Close Project or Phase process also establishes the procedures to investigate and document the reasons for actions taken if a project is terminated before completion. In order to successfully achieve this, the project manager needs to engage all the proper stakeholders in the process.

57. Answer: D.

PMBOK® Guide, pages 112–113, Section 4.5.3; and pages 127–128, Section 4.7.3

> **Monitor and Control Project Work: Outputs**
> .1 Work performance reports
> .2 Change requests
> .3 Project management plan updates
> .4 Project documents updates
>
> **Close Project or Phase: Outputs**
> .1 Project documents updates
> .2 Final product, service, or result transition
> .3 Final report
> .4 Organizational process asset updates

58. Answer: B.

PMBOK® Guide, pages 100–102, Section 4.4.1

> **Manage Project Knowledge: Inputs**
> .1 Project management plan
> .2 Project documents
>> Project documents that can be considered as inputs for this process include, but are not limited to:
>> • Lessons learned register
>> • Project team assignments
>> • Resource breakdown structure
>> • Stakeholder register
> .3 Deliverables
> .4 Enterprise environmental factors
> .5 Organizational process assets

59. Answer: D.

PMBOK® Guide, pages 102–103, Section 4.4.2

Manage Project Knowledge: Tools and Techniques
.1 Expert judgment
.2 Knowledge management
Tools and techniques include, but are not limited to:

- Work shadowing and reverse shadowing;
- Discussion forums such as focus groups;
- Knowledge-sharing events such as seminars and conferences;
- Workshops, including problem-solving sessions and learning reviews designed to identify lessons learned; and
- Storytelling.

.3 Information management
.4 Interpersonal and team skills

60. Answer: B.

PMBOK® Guide, page 104, Section 4.4.3.1

Lessons Learned Register
The lessons learned register can include the category and description of the situation. The lessons learned register may also include the impact, recommendations, and proposed actions associated with the situation. The lessons learned register may record challenges, problems, realized risks and opportunities, or other content as appropriate.

The lessons learned register is created as an output of this process early in the project. Thereafter, it is used as an input and updated as an output in many processes throughout the project. The persons or teams involved in the work are also involved in capturing the lessons learned. Knowledge can be documented using videos, pictures, audios, or other suitable means that ensure the efficiency of the lessons captured.

At the end of a project or phase, the information is transferred to an organizational process asset called a lessons learned repository.

Project Scope Management
(Section 5 of the *PMBOK® Guide*)

61. Answer: D.
PMBOK® Guide, page 137, Section 5.1.3.1

Scope Management Plan
The scope management plan is a component of the project management plan that describes how the scope will be defined, developed, monitored, controlled, and validated. The components of a scope management plan include:
- Process for preparing a project scope statement;
- Process that enables the creation of the WBS from the detailed project scope statement;
- Process that establishes how the scope baseline will be approved and maintained; and
- Process that specifies how formal acceptance of the completed project deliverables will be obtained.

The scope management plan can be formal or informal, broadly framed or highly detailed, based on the needs of the project.

62. Answer: C.
PMBOK® Guide, pages 138–140, Section 5.2

Collect Requirements
The *PMBOK® Guide* does not specifically address product requirements because those are industry specific. Note that *Business Analysis for Practitioners: A Practice Guide* [7] provides more in-depth information about product requirements. The project's success is directly influenced by active stakeholder involvement in the discovery and decomposition of needs into project and product requirements and by the care taken in determining, documenting, and managing the requirements of the product, service, or result of the project. Requirements include conditions or capabilities that are required to be present in a product, service, or result to satisfy an agreement or other formally imposed specification. Requirements include the quantified and documented needs and expectations of the sponsor, customer, and other stakeholders. These requirements need to be elicited, analyzed, and recorded in enough detail to be included in the scope baseline and to be measured once project execution begins. Requirements become the foundation of the WBS. Cost, schedule, quality planning, and procurement are all based on these requirements.

In C, the development of the risk register occurs later in the process.

63. Answer: D.
PMBOK® Guide, page 140, Section 5.2.1

Collect Requirements: Inputs
The stakeholder register is used to identify stakeholders who can provide information on the requirements. It also captures requirements and expectations that stakeholders have for the project.

64. Answer: D.

PMBOK® Guide, pages 148–149, Section 5.2.3.2; and Figure 5-7

Requirements Traceability Matrix

The requirements traceability matrix is a grid that links product requirements from their origin to the deliverables that satisfy them. The implementation of a requirements traceability matrix helps ensure that each requirement adds business value by linking it to the business and project objectives. It provides a means to track requirements throughout the project life cycle, helping to ensure that requirements approved in the requirements documentation are delivered at the end of the project. Finally, it provides a structure for managing changes to the product scope.

Tracing requirements includes, but is not limited to:
- Business needs, opportunities, goals, and objectives;
- Project objectives;
- Project scope and WBS deliverables;
- Product design;
- Product development;
- Test strategy and test scenarios; and
- High-level requirements to more detailed requirements.

Attributes associated with each requirement can be recorded in the requirements traceability matrix. These attributes help define key information about the requirement. Typical attributes used in the requirements traceability matrix may include a unique identifier, a textual description of the requirement, the rationale for inclusion, owner, source, priority, version, current status (such as active, canceled, deferred, added, approved, assigned, completed), and status date. Additional attributes to ensure that the requirement has met stakeholders' satisfaction may include stability, complexity, and acceptance criteria. Figure 5-7 provides an example of a requirements traceability matrix with its associated attributes.

65. Answer: C.

PMBOK® Guide, page 150, Figure 5-8; and page 154, Section 5.3.3

Define Scope: Outputs

Outputs from the Define Scope process are as follows:

.1 Project scope statement

.2 Project document updates

- Assumption log,
- Requirements documentation,
- Requirements traceability matrix, and
- Stakeholder register.

66. Answer: A.

PMBOK® Guide, pages 154–155, Table 5-1, and Section 5.3.3.1

Project Scope Statement

The project scope statement is the description of the project scope, major deliverables, assumptions, and constraints. The project scope statement documents the entire scope, including project and product scope. It describes the project's deliverables in detail. It also provides a common understanding of the project scope among project stakeholders. It may contain explicit scope exclusions that can assist in managing stakeholder expectations. It enables the project team to perform more detailed planning, guides the project team's work during execution, and provides the baseline for evaluating whether requests for changes or additional work are contained within or outside the project's boundaries.

The degree and level of detail to which the project scope statement defines the work that will be performed and the work that is excluded can help determine how well the project management team can control the overall project scope. The detailed project scope statement, either directly or by reference to other documents, includes the following:

- Product scope description. Progressively elaborates the characteristics of the product, service, or result described in the project charter and requirements documentation.
- Deliverables. Any unique and verifiable product, result, or capability to perform a service that is required to be produced to complete a process, phase, or project. Deliverables also include ancillary results, such as project management reports and documentation. These deliverables may be described at a summary level or in great detail.
- Acceptance criteria. A set of conditions that is required to be met before deliverables are accepted.
- Project exclusions. Identify what is excluded from the project; explicitly stating what is out of scope for the project helps manage stakeholders' expectations and can reduce scope creep.

67. Answer: A.

PMBOK® Guide, pages 156–157, Section 5.4

Create WBS

Create WBS is the process of subdividing project deliverables and project work into smaller, more manageable components. The key benefit of this process is that it provides a framework of what has to be delivered. This process is performed once or at predefined points in the project.

The WBS is a hierarchical decomposition of the total scope of work to be carried out by the project team to accomplish the project objectives and create the required deliverables. The WBS organizes and defines the total scope of the project and represents the work specified in the current approved project scope statement.

68. Answer: A.

PMBOK® Guide, page 154, Section 5.3.3.1; page 415, Section 11.2.2.3; and Glossary

Section 5.3.3.1: Project scope statement may contain explicit scope exclusions that can assist in managing stakeholder expectations. Scope exclusions are often a result of project constraints.

Section 11.2.2.3: Constraints may give rise to opportunities through removing or relaxing a limiting factor that affects the execution of a project or process.

Glossary: A limiting factor that affects the execution of a project, program, portfolio, or process.

69. Answer: B.

PMBOK® Guide, pages 150–153, Section 5-3, Figure 5-8

Define Scope: Inputs
.1 Project charter
.2 Project management plan
  • Scope management plan
.3 Project documents
  • Assumption log
  • Requirements documentation
.4 Enterprise environmental factors
.5 Organizational process assets

70. Answer: A.

PMBOK® Guide, pages 156–157, Section 5.4

Create WBS
Create WBS is the process of subdividing project deliverables and project work into smaller, more manageable components. The key benefit of this process is that it provides a framework of what has to be delivered. This process is performed once or at predefined points in the project.

The WBS is a hierarchical decomposition of the total scope of work to be carried out by the project team to accomplish the project objectives and create the required deliverables. The WBS organizes and defines the total scope of the project and represents the work specified in the current approved project scope statement.

71. Answer: B.

PMBOK® Guide, page 161, Section 5.4.3.1

Scope Baseline

WBS. The WBS is a hierarchical decomposition of the total scope of work to be carried out by the project team to accomplish the project objectives and create the required deliverables. Each descending level of the WBS represents an increasingly detailed definition of the project work.

72. Answer: A.

PMBOK® Guide, pages 163–164, Section 5.5

Validate Scope

Validate Scope is the process of formalizing acceptance of the completed project deliverables. The key benefit of this process is that it brings objectivity to the acceptance process and increases the chance of final product, service, or result acceptance by validating each deliverable.

The Validate Scope process differs from the Control Quality process in that the former is primarily concerned with acceptance of the deliverables, while quality control is primarily concerned with correctness of the deliverables and meeting the quality requirements specified for the deliverables. Control Quality is generally performed before Validate Scope, although the two processes may be performed in parallel.

73. Answer: B.

PMBOK® Guide, page 162, Section 5.4.3.1

Scope Baseline

WBS dictionary. The WBS dictionary is a document that provides detailed deliverable, activity, and scheduling information about each component in the WBS.

The WBS dictionary is a document that supports the WBS. Most of the information included in the WBS dictionary is created by other processes and added to this document at a later stage. Information in the WBS dictionary may include, but is not limited to:

- Code of account identifier,
- Description of work,
- Assumptions and constraints,
- Responsible organization,
- Schedule milestones,
- Associated schedule activities,
- Resources required,
- Cost estimates,
- Quality requirements,
- Acceptance criteria,
- Technical references, and
- Agreement information.

74. Answer: D.

PMBOK® Guide, pages 170–171, Section 5.6.3; page 160, Figure 5-14; pages 167–168, Figure 5-17 and Figure 5-18

Control Scope: Outputs
.1 Work performance information
.2 Change requests
.3 Project management plan updates
- Scope management plan
- Scope baseline
- Schedule baseline
- Cost baseline

.4 Project documents updates
- Lessons learned register
- Requirements documentation
- Requirements traceability matrix

75. Answer: C.
PMBOK® Guide, pages 167–168, Section 5.6

Control Scope
Control Scope is the process of monitoring the status of the project and product scope and managing changes to the scope baseline. The key benefit of this process is that the scope baseline is maintained throughout the project. This process is performed throughout the project.

The inputs, tools and techniques, and outputs of this process are depicted in Figure 5-17. Figure 5-18 depicts the data flow diagram of the process.

Controlling the project scope ensures all requested changes and recommended corrective or preventive actions are processed through the Perform Integrated Change Control process (see Section 4.6). Control Scope is also used to manage the actual changes when they occur and is integrated with the other control processes. The uncontrolled expansion to product or project scope without adjustments to time, cost, and resources is referred to as scope creep. Change is inevitable; therefore, some type of change control process is mandatory for every project.

76. Answer D.
PMBOK® Guide, page 148, Section 5.2.3.1

Transition and readiness requirements describe temporary capabilities, such as data conversion and training requirements, needed to transition from the current as-is state to the desired future state.

77. Answer C.
PMBOK® Guide, page 133

In projects with evolving requirements, high risk, or significant uncertainty, the scope is often not understood at the beginning of the project or it evolves during the project. Agile methods deliberately spend less time trying to define and agree on scope in the early stage of the project and spend more time establishing the process for its ongoing discovery and refinement. Many environments with emerging requirements find that there is often a gap between the real business requirements and the business requirements that were originally stated. Therefore, agile methods purposefully build and review prototypes and release versions in order to refine the requirements. As a result, scope is defined and redefined throughout the project. In agile approaches, the requirements constitute the backlog.

Project Schedule Management

(Section 6 of the *PMBOK® Guide*)

78. Answer: B.

PMBOK® Guide, page 185, Section 6.2.2.3

Rolling Wave Planning

Rolling wave planning is an iterative planning technique in which the work to be accomplished in the near term is planned in detail, while work further in the future is planned at a higher level. It is a form of progressive elaboration applicable to work packages, planning packages, and release planning when using an agile or waterfall approach. Therefore, work can exist at various levels of detail depending on where it is in the project life cycle. During early strategic planning when information is less defined, work packages may be decomposed to the known level of detail. As more is known about the upcoming events in the near term, work packages can be decomposed into activities.

79. Answer: A.

PMBOK® Guide, page 189, Section 6.3.2.1

Precedence Diagramming Method

The precedence diagramming method (PDM) is a technique used for constructing a schedule model in which activities are represented by nodes and are graphically linked by one or more logical relationships to show the sequence in which the activities are to be performed.

80. **Answer: D.**

PMBOK® Guide, pages 195–196, Section 6.4

Estimate Activity Durations

Estimate activity durations uses information from the scope of work, required resource types or skill levels, estimated resource quantities, and resource calendars. Other factors that may influence the duration estimates include constraints imposed on the duration, effort involved, or type of resources (e.g., fixed duration, fixed effort or work, fixed number of resources), as well as the schedule network analysis technique used. The inputs for the estimates of duration originate from the person or group on the project team who is most familiar with the nature of the work in the specific activity. The duration estimate is progressively elaborated, and the process considers the quality and availability of the input data. For example, as more detailed and precise data are available about the project engineering and design work, the accuracy and quality of the duration estimates improve.

The specific method for analyzing activity duration does not impact the duration.

81. Answer: A.

PMBOK® Guide, page 215, Section 6.5.2.6

Schedule Compression

Schedule compression techniques are used to shorten or accelerate the schedule duration without reducing the project scope in order to meet schedule constraints, imposed dates, or other schedule objectives. A helpful technique is the negative float analysis. The critical path is the one with the least float. Due to violating a constraint or imposed date, the total float can become negative. Two approaches are crashing and fast tracking:

- **Crashing.** A technique used to shorten the schedule duration for the least incremental cost by adding resources. Examples of crashing include approving overtime, bringing in additional resources, or paying to expedite delivery to activities on the critical path. Crashing works only for activities on the critical path where additional resources will shorten the activity's duration. Crashing does not always produce a viable alternative and may result in increased risk and/or cost.

82. Answer: B.
PMBOK® Guide, page 215, Section 6.5.2.6

Schedule Compression

Schedule compression techniques are used to shorten or accelerate the schedule duration without reducing the project scope in order to meet schedule constraints, imposed dates, or other schedule objectives. A helpful technique is the negative float analysis. The critical path is the one with the least float. Due to violating a constraint or imposed date, the total float can become negative. Two approaches are crashing and fast tracking:

- **Fast tracking.** A schedule compression technique in which activities or phases normally done in sequence are performed in parallel for at least a portion of their duration. An example is constructing the foundation for a building before completing all of the architectural drawings. Fast tracking may result in rework and increased risk. Fast tracking only works when activities can be overlapped to shorten the project duration on the critical path. Using leads in case of schedule acceleration usually increases coordination efforts between the activities concerned and increases quality risk. Fast tracking may also increase project costs.

83. Answer: C.

PMBOK® Guide, pages 191–192, Section 6.3.2.2

Dependency Determination and Integration
Dependencies may be characterized by the following
attributes: mandatory or discretionary, internal or
external (as described below). Dependency has four
attributes, but two can be applicable at the same time in
the following ways: mandatory external dependencies,
mandatory internal dependencies, discretionary external
dependencies, or discretionary internal dependencies.

- **Mandatory dependencies.** Mandatory
  dependencies are those that are legally or
  contractually required or inherent in the nature of
  the work. Mandatory dependencies often involve
  physical limitations, such as on a construction
  project, where it is impossible to erect the
  superstructure until after the foundation has been
  built, or on an electronics project, where a prototype
  has to be built before it can be tested. Mandatory
  dependencies are sometimes referred to as hard
  logic or hard dependencies. Technical dependencies
  may not be mandatory. The project team determines
  which dependencies are mandatory during the
  process of sequencing the activities. Mandatory
  dependencies should not be confused with assigning
  schedule constraints in the scheduling tool.
- **Discretionary dependencies.** Discretionary
  dependencies are sometimes referred to as preferred
  logic, preferential logic, or soft logic. Discretionary
  dependencies are established based on knowledge
  of best practices within a particular application
  area or some unusual aspect of the project where
  a specific sequence is desired, even though there
  may be other acceptable sequences. For example,
  generally accepted best practices recommend that
  during construction, the electrical work should start
  after finishing the plumbing work. This order is
  not mandatory and both activities may occur at the
  same time (in parallel), but performing the activities
  in sequential order reduces the overall project
  risk. Discretionary dependencies should be fully
  documented since they can create arbitrary total

float values and can limit later scheduling options. When fast tracking techniques are employed, these discretionary dependencies should be reviewed and considered for modification or removal. The project team determines which dependencies are discretionary during the process of sequencing the activities.

- **External dependencies.** External dependencies involve a relationship between project activities and non-project activities. These dependencies are usually outside of the project team's control. For example, the testing activity in a software project may be dependent on the delivery of hardware from an external source, or governmental environmental hearings may need to be held before site preparation can begin on a construction project. The project management team determines which dependencies are external during the process of sequencing the activities.

- **Internal dependencies.** Internal dependencies involve a precedence relationship between project activities and are generally inside the project team's control. For example, if the team cannot test a machine until they assemble it, there is an internal mandatory dependency. The project management team determines which dependencies are internal during the process of sequencing the activities.

84. Answer: D.

PMBOK® Guide, pages 183–184, Figure 6-5, Section 6.2.1

> **Define Activities: Inputs**
> .1 Schedule Management Plan
> .2 Scope Baseline
> .3 Enterprise Environmental Factors
> .4 Organizational Process Assets

85. Answer: C.

PMBOK® Guide, page 217, Section 6.5.3.2; page 219, Figure 6-21

> **Project Schedule**
> Also known as Gantt charts, bar charts represent schedule information where activities are listed on the vertical axis, dates are shown on the horizontal axis, and activity durations are shown as horizontal bars placed according to start and finish dates. Bar charts are relatively easy to read and are commonly used. Depending on the audience, float can be depicted or not. For control and management communications, the broader, more comprehensive summary activity is used between milestones or across multiple interdependent work packages and is displayed in bar chart reports.

86. Answer: C.

PMBOK® Guide, pages 189–190, Section 6.3.2.1

> **Precedence Diagramming Method**
> The precedence diagramming method (PDM) is a technique used for constructing a schedule model in which activities are represented by nodes and are graphically linked by one or more logical relationships to show the sequence in which the activities are to be performed. PDM includes four types of dependencies or logical relationships. A predecessor activity is an activity that logically comes before a dependent activity in a schedule. A successor activity is a dependent activity that logically comes after another activity in a schedule.

87. Answer: B.

PMBOK® Guide, page 210–211, Section 6.5.2.2

Critical Path Method

The critical path method is used to estimate the minimum project duration and determine the amount of scheduling flexibility on the logical network paths within the schedule model. This schedule network analysis technique calculates the early start, early finish, late start, and late finish dates for all activities without regard for any resource limitations by performing a forward and backward pass analysis through the schedule network, as shown in Figure 6-16. In this example, the longest path includes activities A, C, and D, and therefore, the sequence of A-C-D is the critical path. The critical path is the sequence of activities that represents the longest path through a project, which determines the shortest possible project duration. The resulting early and late start and finish dates are not necessarily the project schedule; rather, they indicate the time periods within which the activity could be executed, using the parameters entered in the schedule model for activity durations, logical relationships, leads, lags, and other known constraints. The critical path method is used to calculate the amount of scheduling flexibility on the logical network paths within the schedule model.

On any network path, the schedule flexibility is measured by the amount of time that a schedule activity can be delayed or extended from its early start date without delaying the project finish date or violating a schedule constraint, and is termed *total float*. A CPM critical path is normally characterized by zero total float on the critical path. As implemented with PDM sequencing, critical paths may have positive, zero, or negative total float depending on constraints applied.

88. Answer: C.
PMBOK® Guide, page 211, Section 6.5.2.3

Resource Optimization Techniques
Resource optimization is used to adjust the start and finish dates of activities to adjust planned resource use to be equal to or less than resource availability. Examples of resource optimization techniques that can be used to adjust the schedule model due to demand and supply of resources include, but are not limited to:

- **Resource leveling.** A technique in which start and finish dates are adjusted based on resource constraints with the goal of balancing the demand for resources with the available supply. Resource leveling can be used when shared or critically required resources are available only at certain times or in limited quantities, or are over-allocated, such as when a resource has been assigned to two or more activities during the same time period (as shown in Figure 6-17), or there is a need to keep resource usage at a constant level. Resource leveling can often cause the original critical path to change. Available float is used for leveling resources. Consequently, the critical path through the project schedule may change.

- **Resource smoothing.** A technique that adjusts the activities of a schedule model such that the requirements for resources on the project do not exceed certain predefined resource limits. In resource smoothing, as opposed to resource leveling, the project's critical path is not changed and the completion date may not be delayed. In other words, activities may only be delayed within their free and total float. Resource smoothing may not be able to optimize all resources.

89. Answer: D.
PMBOK® Guide, page 192, Section 6.3.2.3

Leads and Lags
A lead is the amount of time a successor activity can be advanced with respect to a predecessor activity. For example, on a project to construct a new office building, the landscaping could be scheduled to start two weeks prior to the scheduled punch list completion. This would be shown as a finish-to-start with a two-week lead as shown in Figure 6-10. Lead is often represented as a negative value for lag in scheduling software.

A lag is the amount of time a successor activity will be delayed with respect to a predecessor activity. For example, a technical writing team may begin editing the draft of a large document 15 days after they begin writing it. This can be shown as a start-to-start relationship with a 15-day lag, as shown in Figure 6-10. Lag can also be represented in project schedule network diagrams as shown in Figure 6-11 in the relationship between activities H and I (as indicated by the nomenclature SS+10 [start-to-start plus 10 days lag] even though the offset is not shown relative to a time scale).

90. Answer: A.
PMBOK® Guide, page 201, Section 6.4.2.4; and Glossary

Three-Point Estimating
The accuracy of single-point duration estimates may be improved by considering estimation uncertainty and risk. Using three-point estimates helps define an approximate range for an activity's duration as follows:

- **Most likely (tM).** This estimate is based on the duration of the activity, given the resources likely to be assigned, their productivity, realistic expectations of availability for the activity, dependencies on other participants, and interruptions.
- **Optimistic (tO).** The activity duration based on analysis of the best-case scenario for the activity.
- **Pessimistic (tP).** The duration based on analysis of the worst-case scenario for the activity. Depending on the assumed distribution of values within the range of the three estimates, the expected duration, tE, can be calculated. One commonly used formula is triangular distribution: $tE = (tO + tM + tP) / 3$. Triangular distribution is used when there are insufficient historical data or when using judgmental data. Duration estimates based on three points with an assumed distribution provide an expected duration and clarify the range of uncertainty around the expected duration.

91. Answer: A.
PMBOK® Guide, page 200, Section 6.4.2.2

Analogous Estimating
Analogous estimating is a technique for estimating the duration or cost of an activity or a project using historical data from a similar activity or project. Analogous estimating uses parameters from a previous, similar project, such as duration, budget, size, weight, and complexity, as the basis for estimating the same parameter or measure for a future project. When estimating durations, this technique relies on the actual duration of previous, similar projects as the basis for estimating the duration of the current project. It is a gross value-estimating approach, sometimes adjusted for known differences in project complexity. Analogous duration estimating is frequently used to estimate project duration when there is a limited amount of detailed information about the project. Analogous estimating is generally less costly and less time-consuming than other techniques, but it is also less accurate. Analogous duration estimates can be applied to a total project or to segments of a project and may be used in conjunction with other estimating methods. Analogous estimating is most reliable when the previous activities are similar in fact and not just in appearance, and the project team members preparing the estimates have the needed expertise.

92. Answer: C.

PMBOK® Guide, pages 244–245, Section 7.2.2.5

Three-Point Estimating

...

Depending on the assumed distribution of values within the range of the three estimates, the expected duration, *tE*, can be calculated using a formula. Two commonly used formulas are triangular and beta distributions. The formulas are:

- **Triangular distribution.** $cE = (cO + cM + cP) / 3$
- **Beta distribution** $cE = (cO + 4cM + cP) / 6$

93. Answer: B.

PMBOK® Guide, pages 244–245, Section 7.2.2.5

Three-Point Estimating

...

The accuracy of single-point duration estimates may be improved by considering estimation uncertainty and risk. Using three-point estimates helps define an approximate range for an activity's duration:

- **Most likely (tM).** This estimate is based on the duration of the activity, given the resources likely to be assigned, their productivity, realistic expectations of availability for the activity, dependencies on other participants, and interruptions.
- **Optimistic (tO).** The activity duration based on analysis of the best-case scenario for the activity.
- **Pessimistic (tP).** The duration based on analysis of the worst-case scenario for the activity. Depending on the assumed distribution of values within the range of the three estimates, the expected duration, tE, can be calculated. One commonly used formula is triangular distribution: tE = (tO + tM + tP) / 3. Triangular distribution is used when there are insufficient historical data or when using judgmental data. Duration estimates based on three points with an assumed distribution provide an expected duration and clarify the range of uncertainty around the expected duration.

94. Answer: A.

PMBOK® Guide, page 201, Section 6.4.2.4

Three-Point Estimating

...

The accuracy of single-point duration estimates may be improved by considering estimation uncertainty and risk. Using three-point estimates helps define an approximate range for an activity's duration:

- **Most likely (tM).** This estimate is based on the duration of the activity, given the resources likely to be assigned, their productivity, realistic expectations of availability for the activity, dependencies on other participants, and interruptions.
- **Optimistic (tO).** The activity duration based on analysis of the best-case scenario for the activity.
- **Pessimistic (tP).** The duration based on analysis of the worst-case scenario for the activity. Depending on the assumed distribution of values within the range of the three estimates, the expected duration, tE, can be calculated. One commonly used formula is triangular distribution: tE = (tO + tM + tP) / 3. Triangular distribution is used when there are insufficient historical data or when using judgmental data. Duration estimates based on three points with an assumed distribution provide an expected duration and clarify the range of uncertainty around the expected duration.

95. Answer: A.
PMBOK® Guide, pages 210–211, Section 6.5.2.2

Critical Path Method
The critical path method, which is a method used to estimate the minimum project duration and determine the amount of scheduling flexibility on the logical network paths within the schedule model. This schedule network analysis technique calculates the early start, early finish, late start, and late finish dates for all activities without regard for any resource limitations by performing a forward and backward pass analysis through the schedule network, as shown in Figure 6-18. In this example, the longest path includes activities A, C, and D, and therefore, the sequence of A-C-D is the critical path. The critical path is the sequence of activities that represents the longest path through a project, which determines the shortest possible project duration.

On any network path, the schedule flexibility is measured by the amount of time that a schedule activity can be delayed or extended from its early start date without delaying the project finish date or violating a schedule constraint, and is termed *total float*. A CPM critical path is normally characterized by zero total float on the critical path. As implemented with PDM sequencing, critical paths may have positive, zero, or negative total float depending on constraints applied. Any activity on the critical path is called a critical path activity. Positive total float is caused when the backward pass is calculated from a schedule constraint that is later than the early finish date that has been calculated during forward pass calculation. Negative total float is caused when a constraint on the late dates is violated by duration and logic. Schedule networks may have multiple near-critical paths. Many software packages allow the user to define the parameters used to determine the critical path(s). Adjustments to activity durations (if more resources or less scope can be arranged), logical relationships (if the relationships were discretionary to begin with), leads and lags, or other schedule constraints may be necessary to produce network paths with a zero or positive total float. Once the total float for a network path has been calculated, then the free float—the amount of time that a schedule activity can be delayed without delaying the early start date of any successor or violating a schedule constraint—can also be determined. For example, the free float for Activity B, in Figure 6-18, is five days.

96. Answer: B.

PMBOK® Guide, pages 210–211, Section 6.5.2.2

Critical Path Method

The critical path method, which is a method used to estimate the minimum project duration and determine the amount of scheduling flexibility on the logical network paths within the schedule model. This schedule network analysis technique calculates the early start, early finish, late start, and late finish dates for all activities without regard for any resource limitations by performing a forward and backward pass analysis through the schedule network, as shown in Figure 6-18. In this example, the longest path includes activities A, C, and D, and therefore, the sequence of A-C-D is the critical path. The critical path is the sequence of activities that represents the longest path through a project, which determines the shortest possible project duration.

On any network path, the schedule flexibility is measured by the amount of time that a schedule activity can be delayed or extended from its early start date without delaying the project finish date or violating a schedule constraint, and is termed *total float*. A CPM critical path is normally characterized by zero total float on the critical path. As implemented with PDM sequencing, critical paths may have positive, zero, or negative total float depending on constraints applied. Any activity on the critical path is called a critical path activity. Positive total float is caused when the backward pass is calculated from a schedule constraint that is later than the early finish date that has been calculated during forward pass calculation. Negative total float is caused when a constraint on the late dates is violated by duration and logic. Schedule networks may have multiple near-critical paths. Many software packages allow the user to define the parameters used to determine the critical path(s). Adjustments to activity durations (if more resources or less scope can be arranged), logical relationships (if the relationships were discretionary to begin with), leads and lags, or other schedule constraints may be necessary to produce network paths with a zero or positive total float. Once the total float for a network path has been calculated, then the free float—the amount of time that a schedule activity can be delayed without delaying the early start date of any successor or violating a schedule constraint—can also be determined. For example, the free float for Activity B, in Figure 6-18, is five days.

97. Answer: A.

PMBOK® Guide, page 215, Section 6.5.2.6; and Glossary

Schedule Compression

Schedule compression techniques are used to shorten or accelerate the schedule duration without reducing the project scope in order to meet schedule constraints, imposed dates, or other schedule objectives. A helpful technique is the negative float analysis. The critical path is the one with the least float. Due to violating a constraint or imposed date, the total float can become negative. Schedule compression techniques are compared in Figure 6-19 and include:

- **Crashing.** A technique used to shorten the schedule duration for the least incremental cost by adding resources. Examples of crashing include approving overtime, bringing in additional resources, or paying to expedite delivery to activities on the critical path. Crashing works only for activities on the critical path where additional resources will shorten the activity's duration. Crashing does not always produce a viable alternative and may result in increased risk and/or cost.

98. Answer: B.

PMBOK® Guide, pages 210–211, Section 6.5.2.2; and Figure 6-16

Critical Path Method

The critical path method, which is a method used to estimate the minimum project duration and determine the amount of scheduling flexibility on the logical network paths within the schedule model. This schedule network analysis technique calculates the early start, early finish, late start, and late finish dates for all activities without regard for any resource limitations by performing a forward and backward pass analysis through the schedule network, as shown in Figure 6-16. In this example, the longest path includes activities A, C, and D, and therefore, the sequence of A-C-D is the critical path. The critical path is the sequence of activities that represents the longest path through a project, which determines the shortest possible project duration. The resulting early and late start and finish dates are not necessarily the project schedule; rather, they indicate the time periods within which the activity could be executed, using the parameters entered in the schedule model for activity durations, logical relationships, leads, lags, and other known constraints. The critical path method is used to calculate the amount of scheduling flexibility on the logical network paths within the schedule model.

99. Answer: B.

PMBOK® Guide, pages 210–211, Section 6.5.2.2; and Figure 6-16

Critical Path Method

…

On any network path, the schedule flexibility is measured by the amount of time that a schedule activity can be delayed or extended from its early start date without delaying the project finish date or violating a schedule constraint, and is termed *total float*. A CPM critical path is normally characterized by zero total float on the critical path. As implemented with PDM sequencing, critical paths may have positive, zero, or negative total float depending on constraints applied. Any activity on the critical path is called a critical path activity. Positive total float is caused when the backward pass is calculated from a schedule constraint that is later than the early finish date that has been calculated during forward pass calculation. Negative total float is caused when a constraint on the late dates is violated by duration and logic. Schedule networks may have multiple near-critical paths. Many software packages allow the user to define the parameters used to determine the critical path(s). Adjustments to activity durations (if more resources or less scope can be arranged), logical relationships (if the relationships were discretionary to begin with), leads and lags, or other schedule constraints may be necessary to produce network paths with a zero or positive total float. Once the total float for a network path has been calculated, then the free float—the amount of time that a schedule activity can be delayed without delaying the early start date of any successor or violating a schedule constraint—can also be determined. For example, the free float for Activity B, in Figure 6-18, is five days.

100. Answer: B.

PMBOK® Guide, page 222, Section 6.6

Control Schedule is the process of monitoring the
status of the project to update the project schedule and
managing changes to the schedule baseline. The key
benefit of this process is that the schedule baseline
is maintained throughout the project. This process is
performed throughout the project.

Project Cost Management
(Section 7 of the *PMBOK® Guide*)

101. Answer: B.
PMBOK® Guide, page 231, Introduction; and page 232, Figure 7-1

Project Cost Management
Project Cost Management includes the processes involved in planning, estimating, budgeting, financing, funding, managing, and controlling costs so that the project can be completed within the approved budget.

The Project Cost Management processes are:
7.1 Plan Cost Management—The process of defining how the project costs will be estimated, budgeted, managed, monitored, and controlled.
7.2 Estimate Costs—The process of developing an approximation of the monetary resources needed to complete project work.
7.3 Determine Budget—The process of aggregating the estimated costs of individual activities or work packages to establish an authorized cost baseline.
7.4 Control Costs—The process of monitoring the status of the project to update the project costs and manage changes to the cost baseline.

102. **Answer: A.**
PMBOK® Guide, pages 238–239, Section 7.1.3.1

Cost Management Plan
The cost management plan is a component of the project management plan and describes how the project costs will be planned, structured, and controlled. The cost management processes and their associated tools and techniques are documented in the cost management plan.

For example, the cost management plan can establish the following:

- **Units of measure.** Each unit used in measurements (such as staff hours, staff days, or weeks for time measures; meters, liters, tons, kilometers, or cubic yards for quantity measures; or lump sum in currency form) is defined for each of the resources.
- **Level of precision.** The degree to which activity cost estimates will be rounded up or down (e.g., US$100.49 to US$100, or US$995.59 to US$1,000), based on the scope of the activities and magnitude of the project.
- **Level of accuracy.** The acceptable range (e.g., ±10%) used in determining realistic activity cost estimates is specified, and may include an amount for contingencies.
- **Organizational procedures links...**
- **Control thresholds.** Variance thresholds for monitoring cost performance may be specified to indicate an agreed-upon amount of variation to be allowed before some action needs to be taken. Thresholds are typically expressed as percentage deviations from the baseline plan.
- **Rules of performance measurement**...
- **Reporting formats...**
- **Process descriptions**...
- **Additional details**...

103. Answer: C.
PMBOK® Guide, pages 240–241, Section 7.2

Estimate Costs

A cost estimate is a quantitative assessment of the likely costs for resources required to complete the activity. It is a prediction that is based on the information known at a given point in time. Cost estimates include the identification and consideration of costing alternatives to initiate and complete the project. Cost trade-offs and risks should be considered, such as make versus buy, buy versus lease, and the sharing of resources in order to achieve optimal costs for the project.

Cost estimates are generally expressed in units of some currency (i.e., dollars, euros, yen, etc.), although in some instances other units of measure, such as staff hours or staff days, are used to facilitate comparisons by eliminating the effects of currency fluctuations.

Cost estimates should be reviewed and refined during the course of the project to reflect additional detail as it becomes available and assumptions are tested. The accuracy of a project estimate will increase as the project progresses through the project life cycle. For example, a project in the initiation phase may have a rough order of magnitude (ROM) estimate in the range of −25% to +75%. Later in the project, as more information is known, definitive estimates could narrow the range of accuracy to −5% to +10%. In some organizations, there are guidelines for when such refinements can be made and the degree of confidence or accuracy that is expected.

Costs are estimated for all resources that will be charged to the project. This includes, but is not limited to, labor, materials, equipment, services, and facilities, as well as special categories such as an inflation allowance, cost of financing, or contingency costs. Cost estimates may be presented at the activity level or in summary form.

104. Answer: D.

PMBOK® Guide, page 241, Section 7.2

Estimate Costs

Costs are estimated for all resources that will be charged to the project. This includes, but is not limited to, labor, materials, equipment, services, and facilities, as well as special categories such as an inflation allowance, cost of financing, or contingency costs. A cost estimate is a quantitative assessment of the likely costs for resources required to complete the activity. Cost estimates may be presented at the activity level or in summary form.

105. Answer: C.

PMBOK® Guide, page 244, Section 7.2.2.3

Parametric Estimating

Parametric estimating uses a statistical relationship between relevant historical data and other variables (e.g., square footage in construction) to calculate a cost estimate for project work. This technique can produce higher levels of accuracy depending on the sophistication and underlying data built into the model. Parametric cost estimates can be applied to a total project or to segments of a project, in conjunction with other estimating methods.

106. Answer: B.

PMBOK® Guide, page 244, Section 7.2.2.2

Analogous Estimating

Analogous cost estimating uses values, or attributes, of a previous project that are similar to the current project. Values and attributes of the projects may include, but are not limited to, scope, cost, budget, duration, and measures of scale (e.g., size, weight). Comparison of these project values, or attributes, becomes the basis for estimating the same parameter or measurement for the current project.

107. Answer: C.

PMBOK® Guide, page 248, Section 7.3; and pages 257–259, Section 7.4

Determine Budget
Determine Budget is the process of aggregating the estimated costs of individual activities or work packages to establish an authorized cost baseline. The key benefit of this process is that it determines the cost baseline against which project performance can be monitored and controlled.

Control Costs
Control Costs is the process of monitoring the status of the project to update the project costs and managing changes to the cost baseline. The key benefit of this process is that it provides the means to recognize variance from the plan in order to take corrective action and minimize risk.

The key to effective cost control is the management of the approved cost baseline and the changes to that baseline.

Project cost control includes:
- Influencing the factors that create changes to the authorized cost baseline...

108. Answer: B.

PMBOK® Guide, pages 254–255, Section 7.3.3.1, Figure 7-8 and Figure 7-9

Cost Baseline

The cost baseline is the approved version of the time-phased project budget, excluding any management reserves, which can only be changed through formal change control procedures and is used as a basis for comparison to actual results. It is developed as a summation of the approved budgets for the different schedule activities. Figure 7-8 illustrates the various components of the project budget and cost baseline. Activity cost estimates for the various project activities, along with any contingency reserves for these activities, are aggregated into their associated work package costs. The work package cost estimates, along with any contingency reserves estimated for the work packages, are aggregated into control accounts. The summation of the control accounts make up the cost baseline. Since the cost estimates that make up the cost baseline are directly tied to the schedule activities, this enables a time-phased view of the cost baseline, which is typically displayed in the form of an S-curve, as is illustrated in Figure 7-9.

Management reserves are added to the cost baseline to produce the project budget. As changes warranting the use of management reserves arise, the change control process is used to obtain approval to move the applicable management reserve funds into the cost baseline.

109. Answer: D.
PMBOK® Guide, pages 257–259, Section 7.4

Control Costs
Project cost control includes:
- Influencing the factors that create changes to the authorized cost baseline;
- Ensuring that all change requests are acted on in a timely manner;
- Managing the actual changes when and as they occur;
- Ensuring that cost expenditures do not exceed the authorized funding by period, by WBS component, by activity, and in total for the project;
- Monitoring cost performance to isolate and understand variances from the approved cost baseline;
- Monitoring work performance against funds expended;
- Preventing unapproved changes from being included in the reported cost or resource usage;
- Informing appropriate stakeholders of all approved changes and associated costs; and
- Bringing expected cost overruns within acceptable limits.

110. Answer: B.
PMBOK® Guide, pages 261–265, Section 7.4.2.2; and Figure 7-12

A good understanding of the earned value analysis is required to properly interpret this graph. Review the entire Section 7.4.2.2 for a full description.

111. Answer: C.

PMBOK® Guide, page 265, Section 7.4.2.2

Forecasting

The project manager's manual EAC is quickly compared with a range of calculated EACs representing various risk scenarios. When calculating EAC values, the cumulative CPI and SPI values are typically used. While EVM data quickly provide many statistical EACs, only three of the more common methods are described as follows:

- **EAC forecast for ETC work performed at the budgeted rate.** This EAC method accepts the actual project performance to date (whether favorable or unfavorable) as represented by the actual costs, and predicts that all future ETC work will be accomplished at the budgeted rate. When actual performance is unfavorable, the assumption that future performance will improve should be accepted only when supported by project risk analysis. *Equation:* $EAC = AC + (BAC - EV)$

112. Answer: A.

PMBOK® Guide, pages 264–265, Section 7.4.2.2

Forecasting

The project manager's manual EAC is quickly compared with a range of calculated EACs representing various risk scenarios. When calculating EAC values, the cumulative CPI and SPI values are typically used. While EVM data quickly provide many statistical EACs, only three of the more common methods are described as follows:

- **EAC forecast for ETC work performed at the present CPI.** This method assumes that what the project has experienced to date can be expected to continue in the future. The ETC work is assumed to be performed at the same cumulative cost performance index (CPI) as that incurred by the project to date. *Equation:* $EAC = BAC/CPI$

113. Answer: D.
PMBOK® Guide, page 265, Section 7.4.2.2

Forecasting
The project manager's manual EAC is quickly compared with a range of calculated EACs representing various risk scenarios. When calculating EAC values, the cumulative CPI and SPI values are typically used. While EVM data quickly provide many statistical EACs, only three of the more common methods are described as follows:

- **EAC forecast for ETC work considering both SPI and CPI factors.** In this forecast, the ETC work will be performed at an efficiency rate that considers both the cost and schedule performance indices. This method is most useful when the project schedule is a factor impacting the ETC effort. Variations of this method weight the CPI and SPI at different values (e.g., 80/20, 50/50, or some other ratio) according to the project manager's judgment. *Equation:* $EAC = AC + [(BAC - EV)/(CPI \times SPI)]$

114. Answer: B.
PMBOK® Guide, page 265, Section 7.4.2.2; and page 267, Table 7-1

Forecasting
The project manager's manual EAC is quickly compared with a range of calculated EACs representing various risk scenarios. When calculating EAC values, the cumulative CPI and SPI values are typically used. While EVM data quickly provide many statistical EACs, only three of the more common methods are described as follows:

- **EAC forecast for ETC work performed at the present CPI.** This method assumes what the project has experienced to date can be expected to continue in the future. The ETC work is assumed to be performed at the same cumulative cost performance index (CPI) as that incurred by the project to date. *Equation:* $EAC = BAC/CPI$

Equation: $VAC = BAC - EAC$

115. Answer: A.

PMBOK® Guide, page 265, Section 7.4.2.2; and page 267, Table 7-1

Forecasting

...

The project manager's manual EAC is quickly compared with a range of calculated EACs representing various risk scenarios. When calculating EAC values, the cumulative CPI and SPI values are typically used. While EVM data quickly provide many statistical EACs, only three of the more common methods are described as follows:

- **EAC forecast for ETC work performed at the budgeted rate.** This EAC method accepts the actual project performance to date (whether favorable or unfavorable) as represented by the actual costs, and predicts that all future ETC work will be accomplished at the budgeted rate. When actual performance is unfavorable, the assumption that future performance will improve should be accepted only when supported by project risk analysis.
  Equation: $EAC = AC + (BAC - EV)$

Equation: $ETC = EAC - AC$

116. Answer: C.

PMBOK® Guide, page 266, Section 7.4.2.3; page 268, Figure 7-13; and page 267, Table 7-1

To-Complete Performance Index (TCPI)

The to-complete performance index (TCPI) is a measure of the cost performance that is required to be achieved with the remaining resources in order to meet a specified management goal, expressed as the ratio of the cost to finish the outstanding work to the remaining budget. TCPI is the calculated cost performance index that is achieved on the remaining work to meet a specified management goal, such as the BAC or the EAC. If it becomes obvious that the BAC is no longer viable, the project manager should consider the forecasted EAC. Once approved, the EAC may replace the BAC in the TCPI calculation. The equation for the TCPI based on the BAC: (BAC − EV)/(BAC − AC).

The TCPI is conceptually displayed in Figure 7-13. The equation for the TCPI is shown in the lower left as the work remaining (defined as the BAC minus the EV) divided by the funds remaining (which can be either the BAC minus the AC, or the EAC minus the AC).

If the cumulative CPI falls below the baseline (as shown in Figure 7-13), all future work of the project will need to be performed immediately in the range of the TCPI (BAC) (as reflected in the top line of Figure 7-13) to stay within the authorized BAC. Whether this level of performance is achievable is a judgment call based on a number of considerations, including risk, schedule, and technical performance. This level of performance is displayed as the TCPI (EAC) line. The equation for the TCPI based on the EAC: (BAC − EV)/(EAC − AC). The EVM formulas are provided in Table 7-1.

Equation: $TCPI = (BAC − EV)/(BAC − AC)$

117. Answer: A.

PMBOK® Guide, page 264, Section 7.4.2.2

Forecasting

As the project progresses, the project team may develop a forecast for the estimate at completion (EAC) that may differ from the budget at completion (BAC) based on the project performance. If it becomes obvious that the BAC is no longer viable, the project manager should consider the forecasted EAC. Forecasting the EAC involves making projections of conditions and events in the project's future based on current performance information and other knowledge available at the time of the forecast. Forecasts are generated, updated, and reissued based on work performance data (Section 4.3.3.2) that are provided as the project is executed. The work performance information covers the project's past performance and any information that could impact the project in the future.

EACs are typically based on the actual costs incurred for work completed, plus an estimate to complete (ETC) the remaining work. It is incumbent on the project team to predict what it may encounter to perform the ETC, based on its experience to date.

118. Answer: C.

PMBOK® Guide, pages 260–265, Section 7.4.2.1; and Figure 7-12

Earned Value Management

...

Variances from the approved baseline will also be monitored:

- **Schedule variance.** Schedule variance (SV) is a measure of schedule performance expressed as the difference between the earned value and the planned value. It is the amount by which the project is ahead or behind the planned delivery date, at a given point in time. It is a measure of schedule performance on a project. It is equal to the earned value (EV) minus the planned value (PV). The EVM schedule variance is a useful metric in that it can indicate when a project is falling behind or is ahead of its baseline schedule. The EVM schedule variance will ultimately equal zero when the project is completed because all of the planned values will have been earned. Schedule variance is best used in conjunction with critical path methodology (CPM) scheduling and risk management. *Equation:* $SV = EV - PV$

...

The SV and CV values can be converted to efficiency indicators to reflect the cost and schedule performance of any project for comparison against all other projects or within a portfolio of projects. The variances are useful for determining project status.

- **Schedule performance index.** The schedule performance index (SPI) is a measure of schedule efficiency expressed as the ratio of earned value to planned value. It measures how efficiently the project team is using its time. It is sometimes used in conjunction with the cost performance index (CPI) to forecast the final project completion estimates. An SPI value less than 1.0 indicates less work was completed than was planned. An SPI greater than 1.0 indicates that more work was completed than was planned. Because the SPI measures all project work, the performance on the critical path also needs to be analyzed to determine whether the project will finish ahead of or behind its planned finish date. The SPI is equal to the ratio of the EV to the PV. *Equation:* SPI = EV/PV

...

The three parameters of planned value, earned value, and actual cost can be monitored and reported on both a period-by-period basis (typically weekly or monthly) and on a cumulative basis. Figure 7-12 uses S-curves to display EV data for a project that is performing over budget and behind schedule.

119. Answer: A.

PMBOK® Guide, pages 260–265, Section 7.4.2.1; and Figure 7-12

Earned Value Management

...

Variances from the approved baseline will also be monitored:

...

- **Cost variance.** Cost variance (CV) is the amount of budget deficit or surplus at a given point in time, expressed as the difference between earned value and the actual cost. It is a measure of cost performance on a project. It is equal to the earned value (EV) minus the actual cost (AC). The cost variance at the end of the project will be the difference between the budget at completion (BAC) and the actual amount spent. The CV is particularly critical because it indicates the relationship of physical performance to the costs spent. Negative CV is often difficult for the project to recover. *Equation:* $CV = EV - AC$

The SV and CV values can be converted to efficiency indicators to reflect the cost and schedule performance of any project for comparison against all other projects or within a portfolio of projects. The variances are useful for determining project status.

...

- **Cost performance index.** The cost performance index (CPI) is a measure of the cost efficiency of budgeted resources, expressed as a ratio of earned value to actual cost. It is considered the most critical EVM metric and measures the cost efficiency for the work completed. A CPI value of less than 1.0 indicates a cost overrun for work completed. A CPI value greater than 1.0 indicates a cost underrun of performance to date. The CPI is equal to the ratio of the EV to the AC. The indices are useful for determining project status and providing a basis for estimating project cost and schedule outcome. *Equation:* $CPI = EV/AC$

The three parameters of planned value, earned value, and actual cost can be monitored and reported on both a period-by-period basis (typically weekly or monthly) and on a cumulative basis. Figure 7-12 uses S-curves to display EV data for a project that is performing over budget and behind schedule.

120. Answer: C.
PMBOK® Guide, page 261, Section 7.4.2.2

Data Analysis
Earned value analysis (EVA), sometimes called earned value management (EVM), compares the performance measurement baseline to the actual schedule and cost performance. EVM integrates the scope baseline with the cost baseline and schedule baseline to form the performance measurement baseline. EVM develops and monitors three key dimensions for each work package and control account.

121. Answer: D.

PMBOK® Guide, pages 260–265, Section 7.4.2.2; and Figure 7-12

Earned Value Management

...

Variances from the approved baseline will also be monitored:

- **Schedule variance.** Schedule variance (SV) is a measure of schedule performance expressed as the difference between the earned value and the planned value. It is the amount by which the project is ahead or behind the planned delivery date, at a given point in time. It is a measure of schedule performance on a project. It is equal to the earned value (EV) minus the planned value (PV). The EVM schedule variance is a useful metric in that it can indicate when a project is falling behind or is ahead of its baseline schedule. The EVM schedule variance will ultimately equal zero when the project is completed because all of the planned values will have been earned. Schedule variance is best used in conjunction with critical path methodology (CPM) scheduling and risk management. *Equation:* $SV = EV - PV$

- **Cost variance.** Cost variance (CV) is the amount of budget deficit or surplus at a given point in time, expressed as the difference between earned value and the actual cost. It is a measure of cost performance on a project. It is equal to the earned value (EV) minus the actual cost (AC). The cost variance at the end of the project will be the difference between the budget at completion (BAC) and the actual amount spent. The CV is particularly critical because it indicates the relationship of physical performance to the costs spent. Negative CV is often difficult for the project to recover. *Equation:* $CV = EV - AC$

The SV and CV values can be converted to efficiency indicators to reflect the cost and schedule performance of any project for comparison against all other projects or within a portfolio of projects. The variances are useful for determining project status.

- **Schedule performance index.** The schedule performance index (SPI) is a measure of schedule efficiency expressed as the ratio of earned value to planned value. It measures how efficiently the project team is using its time. It is sometimes used in conjunction with the cost performance index (CPI) to forecast the final project completion estimates. An SPI value less than 1.0 indicates less work was completed than was planned. An SPI greater than 1.0 indicates that more work was completed than was planned. Since the SPI measures all project work, the performance on the critical path also needs to be analyzed to determine whether the project will finish ahead of or behind its planned finish date. The SPI is equal to the ratio of the EV to the PV. *Equation:* SPI $=$ EV/PV

- **Cost performance index.** The cost performance index (CPI) is a measure of the cost efficiency of budgeted resources, expressed as a ratio of earned value to actual cost. It is considered the most critical EVM metric and measures the cost efficiency for the work completed. A CPI value of less than 1.0 indicates a cost overrun for work completed. A CPI value greater than 1.0 indicates a cost underrun of performance to date. The CPI is equal to the ratio of the EV to the AC. The indices are useful for determining project status and providing a basis for estimating project cost and schedule outcome. *Equation:* CPI $=$ EV/AC

The three parameters of planned value, earned value, and actual cost can be monitored and reported on both a period-by-period basis (typically weekly or monthly) and on a cumulative basis. Figure 7-12 uses S-curves to display EV data for a project that is performing over budget and behind schedule.

122. Answer: B.

PMBOK® Guide, page 262, Section 7.4.2.2

Earned Value Management

...

Variances from the approved baseline will also be monitored:

...

- **Cost variance.** Cost variance (CV) is the amount of budget deficit or surplus at a given point in time, expressed as the difference between earned value and the actual cost. It is a measure of cost performance on a project. It is equal to the earned value (EV) minus the actual cost (AC). The cost variance at the end of the project will be the difference between the budget at completion (BAC) and the actual amount spent. The CV is particularly critical because it indicates the relationship of physical performance to the costs spent. Negative CV is often difficult for the project to recover. *Equation:* $CV = EV - AC$

123. Answer: B.
PMBOK® Guide, page 261, Section 7.4.2.2

Earned Value Management

... Earned value management (EVM) develops and monitors three key dimensions for each work package and control account:

...

- **Earned value.** Earned value (EV) is a measure of work performed expressed in terms of the budget authorized for that work. It is the budget associated with the authorized work that has been completed. The EV being measured needs to be related to the PMB, and the EV measured cannot be greater than the authorized PV budget for a component. The EV is often used to calculate the percent complete of a project. Progress measurement criteria should be established for each WBS component to measure work in progress. Project managers monitor EV, both incrementally to determine current status and cumulatively to determine the long-term performance trends.

124. Answer: B.

PMBOK® Guide, page 263, Section 7.4.2.2; and Figure 7-12

Earned Value Management

...

- **Schedule performance index.** The schedule performance index (SPI) is a measure of schedule efficiency expressed as the ratio of earned value to planned value. It measures how efficiently the project team is using its time. It is sometimes used in conjunction with the cost performance index (CPI) to forecast the final project completion estimates. An SPI value less than 1.0 indicates less work was completed than was planned. An SPI greater than 1.0 indicates that more work was completed than was planned. Since the SPI measures all project work, the performance on the critical path also needs to be analyzed to determine whether the project will finish ahead of or behind its planned finish date. The SPI is equal to the ratio of the EV to the PV. *Equation:* SPI = EV/PV

- **Cost performance index.** The cost performance index (CPI) is a measure of the cost efficiency of budgeted resources, expressed as a ratio of earned value to actual cost. It is considered the most critical EVM metric and measures the cost efficiency for the work completed. A CPI value of less than 1.0 indicates a cost overrun for work completed. A CPI value greater than 1.0 indicates a cost underrun of performance to date. The CPI is equal to the ratio of the EV to the AC. The indices are useful for determining project status and providing a basis for estimating project cost and schedule outcome. *Equation:* CPI = EV/AC

The three parameters of planned value, earned value, and actual cost can be monitored and reported on both a period-by-period basis (typically weekly or monthly) and on a cumulative basis. Figure 7-12 uses S-curves to display EV data for a project that is performing over budget and behind schedule.

125. Answer: D.

PMBOK® Guide, pages 260–265, Section 7.4.2.2; and Figure 7-12

Earned Value Management

...

Variances from the approved baseline will also be monitored:

...

- **Cost variance.** Cost variance (CV) is the amount of budget deficit or surplus at a given point in time, expressed as the difference between earned value and the actual cost. It is a measure of cost performance on a project. It is equal to the earned value (EV) minus the actual cost (AC). The cost variance at the end of the project will be the difference between the budget at completion (BAC) and the actual amount spent. The CV is particularly critical because it indicates the relationship of physical performance to the costs spent. Negative CV is often difficult for the project to recover. *Equation:* $CV = EV - AC$

The SV and CV values can be converted to efficiency indicators to reflect the cost and schedule performance of any project for comparison against all other projects or within a portfolio of projects. The variances are useful for determining project status.

...

- **Cost performance index.** The cost performance index (CPI) is a measure of the cost efficiency of budgeted resources, expressed as a ratio of earned value to actual cost. It is considered the most critical EVM metric and measures the cost efficiency for the work completed. A CPI value of less than 1.0 indicates a cost overrun for work completed. A CPI value greater than 1.0 indicates a cost underrun of performance to date. The CPI is equal to the ratio of the EV to the AC. The indices are useful for determining project status and providing a basis for estimating project cost and schedule outcome. *Equation:* $CPI = EV/AC$

The three parameters of planned value, earned value, and actual cost can be monitored and reported on both a period-by-period basis (typically weekly or monthly) and on a cumulative basis. Figure 7-12 uses S-curves to display EV data for a project that is performing over budget and behind schedule.

126. Answer: D.

PMBOK® Guide, pages 260–265, Section 7.4.2.2; and Figure 7-12

Earned Value Management

...

The SV and CV values can be converted to efficiency indicators to reflect the cost and schedule performance of any project for comparison against all other projects or within a portfolio of projects. The variances are useful for determining project status.

- **Schedule performance index.** The schedule performance index (SPI) is a measure of schedule efficiency expressed as the ratio of earned value to planned value. It measures how efficiently the project team is using its time. It is sometimes used in conjunction with the cost performance index (CPI) to forecast the final project completion estimates. An SPI value less than 1.0 indicates less work was completed than was planned. An SPI greater than 1.0 indicates that more work was completed than was planned. Because the SPI measures all project work, the performance on the critical path also needs to be analyzed to determine whether the project will finish ahead of or behind its planned finish date. The SPI is equal to the ratio of the EV to the PV. *Equation:* $SPI = EV/PV$

...

The three parameters of planned value, earned value, and actual cost can be monitored and reported on both a period-by-period basis (typically weekly or monthly) and on a cumulative basis. Figure 7-12 uses S-curves to display EV data for a project that is performing over budget and behind schedule.

Project Quality Management
(Section 8 of the *PMBOK® Guide*)

127. Answer: A.
PMBOK® Guide, Introduction, page 271

Project Quality Management
Project Quality Management includes the processes for incorporating the organization's quality policy regarding planning, managing, and controlling project and product quality requirements in order to meet stakeholders' objectives. Project Quality Management also supports continuous process improvement activities as undertaken on behalf of the performing organization.

128. Answer: A.
PMBOK® Guide, page 274

Project Quality Management
Quality and grade are not the same concepts. Quality as a delivered performance or result is "the degree to which a set of inherent characteristics fulfill requirements" (ISO 9000 [18]). Grade as a design intent is a category assigned to deliverables having the same functional use but different technical characteristics. The project manager and the project management team are responsible for managing the trade-offs associated with delivering the required levels of both quality and grade. While a quality level that fails to meet quality requirements is always a problem, a low-grade product may not be a problem. For example:

- It may not be a problem if a suitable low-grade product (one with a limited number of features) is of high quality (no obvious defects). In this example, the product would be appropriate for its general purpose of use; or
- It may be a problem if a high-grade product (one with numerous features) is of low quality (many defects). In essence, a high-grade feature set would prove ineffective and/or inefficient due to low quality.

129. Answer: A.
PMBOK® Guide, Section 8.3, page 298

Control Quality
The process of monitoring and recording the results of executing the quality management activities to assess performance and ensure the project outputs are complete, correct, and meet customer expectations.

130. Answer: D.
PMBOK® Guide, Section 8.1.2.3, page 282

Data Analysis
Data analysis techniques that can be used for this
process include, but are not limited to:
- **Cost-benefit analysis.** A cost-benefit analysis
  is a financial analysis tool used to estimate the
  strengths and weaknesses of alternatives in order to
  determine the best alternative in terms of benefits
  provided. A cost-benefit analysis will help the project
  manager determine if the planned quality activities
  are cost effective. The primary benefits of meeting
  quality requirements include less rework, higher
  productivity, lower costs, increased stakeholder
  satisfaction, and increased profitability. A cost-benefit
  analysis for each quality activity compares the cost of
  the quality step to the expected benefit.

131. Answer: D.
PMBOK® Guide, pages 300–302, Section 8.3.1; and page 298,
Figure 8-10

The Control Quality process has the following inputs:

Project management plan
- Quality management plan

Project documents
- Lessons learned register
- Quality metrics
- Test and evaluation documents

Approved change requests
Deliverables
Work performance data
Enterprise environmental factors
Organizational process assets

132. **Answer: A.**

PMBOK® Guide, page 286, Section 8.1.3.1

Quality Management Plan

The quality management plan is a component of
the project management plan that describes how
applicable policies, procedures, and guidelines will
be implemented to achieve the quality objectives.
It describes the activities and resources necessary for
the project management team to achieve the quality
objectives set for the project. The quality management
plan may be formal or informal, detailed, or broadly
framed. The style and detail of the quality management
plan are determined by the requirements of the project.
The quality management plan should be reviewed
early in the project to ensure that decisions are based
on accurate information. The benefits of this review
can include a sharper focus on the project's value
proposition, reductions in costs, and less frequent
schedule overruns that are caused by rework.

133. **Answer: C.**

PMBOK® Guide, page 288, Section 8.2, Figure 8-7

Manage Quality

Manage Quality is the process of translating the quality
management plan into executable quality activities
that incorporate the organization's quality policies
into the project. The key benefits of this process are
that it increases the probability of meeting the quality
objectives as well as identifying ineffective processes
and causes of poor quality. Manage Quality uses the
data and results from the Control Quality process to
reflect the overall quality status of the project to the
stakeholders. This process is performed throughout
the project.

134. Answer: D.

PMBOK® Guide, page 271, Section 8, Figure 8-1

Project Quality Management

The cost of quality (COQ) includes all costs incurred over the life of the product by investment in preventing nonconformance to requirements, appraising the product or service for conformance to requirements, and failing to meet requirements (rework). Failure costs are often categorized into internal (found by the project team) and external (found by the customer). Failure costs are also called the cost of poor quality. Section 8.1.2.3 provides some examples to consider in each area. Organizations choose to invest in defect prevention because of the benefits over the life of the product. Because projects are temporary, decisions about the COQ over a product's life cycle are often the concern of portfolio management, program management, the PMO, or operations.

135. Answer: A.

PMBOK® Guide, page 274, Section 8

Project Quality Management

The cost of quality (COQ) includes all costs incurred over the life of the product by investment in preventing nonconformance to requirements, appraising the product or service for conformance to requirements, and failing to meet requirements (rework). Failure costs are often categorized into internal (found by the project team) and external (found by the customer). Failure costs are also called the cost of poor quality. Section 8.1.2.3 provides some examples to consider in each area. Organizations choose to invest in defect prevention because of the benefits over the life of the product. Because projects are temporary, decisions about the COQ over a product's life cycle are often the concern of portfolio management, program management, the PMO, or operations.

136. Answer: C.
PMBOK® Guide, page 304, Section 8.3.2.5

Data Representation
Data representation techniques that can be used for this process include, but are not limited to:

- **Control charts.** Control charts are used to determine whether or not a process is stable or has predictable performance. Upper and lower specification limits are based on the requirements and reflect the maximum and minimum values allowed. Upper and lower control limits are different from specification limits. The control limits are determined using standard statistical calculations and principles to ultimately establish the natural capability for a stable process. The project manager and appropriate stakeholders may use the statistically calculated control limits to identify the points at which corrective action will be taken to prevent performance that remains outside the control limits. Control charts can be used to monitor various types of output variables. Although used most frequently to track repetitive activities required for producing manufactured lots, control charts may also be used to monitor cost and schedule variances, volume, frequency of scope changes, or other management results to help determine if the project management processes are in control.

137. Answer: A.
PMBOK® Guide, page 304, Section 8.3.2.5

Data Representation
Data representation techniques that can be used for this process include, but are not limited to:
- **Control charts.** Control charts are used to determine whether or not a process is stable or has predictable performance. Upper and lower specification limits are based on the requirements and reflect the maximum and minimum values allowed. Upper and lower control limits are different from specification limits. The control limits are determined using standard statistical calculations and principles to ultimately establish the natural capability for a stable process. The project manager and appropriate stakeholders may use the statistically calculated control limits to identify the points at which corrective action will be taken to prevent performance that remains outside the control limits. Control charts can be used to monitor various types of output variables. Although used most frequently to track repetitive activities required for producing manufactured lots, control charts may also be used to monitor cost and schedule variances, volume, frequency of scope changes, or other management results to help determine if the project management processes are in control.

138. Answer: B.
PMBOK® Guide, page 599, Section 4.3

Manage Quality
Manage quality is the process of auditing the quality requirements and the results from quality control measurements to ensure that appropriate quality standards and operational definitions are used.
The key benefit of this process is that it facilitates the improvement of quality processes.

139. Answer: B.

PMBOK® Guide, page 282, Section 8.1.2.3

Data Analysis

Data analysis techniques that can be used for this process include, but are not limited to:

- **Cost-benefit analysis.** A cost-benefit analysis is a financial analysis tool used to estimate the strengths and weaknesses of alternatives in order to determine the best alternative in terms of benefits provided. A cost-benefit analysis will help the project manager determine if the planned quality activities are cost effective. The primary benefits of meeting quality requirements include less rework, higher productivity, lower costs, increased stakeholder satisfaction, and increased profitability. A cost-benefit analysis for each quality activity compares the cost of the quality step to the expected benefit.

140. Answer: D.

PMBOK® Guide, page 281, Section 8.1.2.2

Data Gathering

Data gathering techniques that can be used for this process include, but are not limited to:

- **Benchmarking.** Benchmarking involves comparing actual or planned project practices or the project's quality standards to those of comparable projects to identify best practices, generate ideas for improvement, and provide a basis for measuring performance. Benchmarked projects may exist within the performing organization or outside of it, or can be within the same application area or other application area. Benchmarking allows for analogies from projects in a different application area or different industries to be made.

141. Answer: A.
PMBOK® Guide, page 275

Trends and Emerging Practices in Project Quality Management
Continual improvement. The plan-do-check-act (PDCA) cycle is the basis for quality improvement as defined by Shewhart and modified by Deming. In addition, quality improvement initiatives such as total quality management (TQM), Six Sigma, and Lean Six Sigma may improve both the quality of project management, as well as the quality of the end product, service, or result.

142. Answer: A.
PMBOK® Guide, page 293, Section 8.2.2.4

Data Representation
Data representation techniques that can be used for this process include, but are not limited to:
- **Affinity diagrams.** Described in Section 5.2.2.5. Affinity diagrams can organize potential causes of defects into groups showing areas that should be focused on the most.
- **Affinity diagrams.** Affinity diagrams allow large numbers of ideas to be classified into groups for review and analysis.

143. Answer: D.

PMBOK® Guide, page 276, Introduction

Tailoring Considerations

Each project is unique; therefore, the project manager will need to tailor the way Project Quality Management processes are applied. Considerations for tailoring include, but are not limited to the following:

- **Policy compliance and auditing.** What quality policies and procedures exist in the organization? What quality tools, techniques, and templates are used in the organization?
- **Standards and regulatory compliance.** Are there any specific quality standards in the industry that need to be applied? Are there any specific governmental, legal, or regulatory constraints that need to be taken into consideration?
- **Continuous improvement.** How will quality improvement be managed in the project? Is it managed at the organizational level or at the level of each project?
- **Stakeholder engagement.** Is there a collaborative environment for stakeholders and suppliers?

144. Answer: B.

PMBOK® Guide, page 565 and Table 1-4

Planning Process Group
The Planning Process Group consists of those processes performed to establish the total scope of the effort, define and refine the objectives, and develop the course of action required to attain those objectives. The Planning processes develop the project management plan and the project documents that will be used to carry out the project.
...
Table 1-4 reflects the mapping of the 47 project management processes within the five Project Management Process Groups and the 10 Knowledge Areas.

Plan Quality Management—The process of identifying quality requirements and/or standards for the project and its deliverables and documenting how the project will demonstrate compliance with quality requirements.

Project Resource Management
(Section 9 of the *PMBOK® Guide*)

145. Answer: D.
PMBOK® Guide, page 307, Introduction; and page 308, Figure 9-1

Project Resource Management Processes
Figure 9-1 provides an overview of the Project Resource Management processes, which are as follows:

9.1 Plan Resource Management—The process of defining how to estimate, acquire, manage, and utilize physical and team resources.

9.2 Estimate Activity Resources—The process of estimating team resources and the type and quantities of material, equipment, and supplies necessary to perform project work.

9.3 Acquire Resources—The process of obtaining team members, facilities, equipment, materials, supplies, and other resources necessary to complete project work.

9.4 Develop Team—The process of improving competencies, team member interaction, and the overall team environment to enhance project performance.

9.5 Manage Team—The process of tracking team member performance, providing feedback, resolving issues, and managing team changes to optimize project performance.

9.6 Control Resources—The process of ensuring that the physical resources assigned and allocated to the project are available as planned, as well as monitoring the planned versus actual use of resources, and performing corrective action as necessary.

146. **Answer: C.**

PMBOK® Guide, pages 316–317, Section 9.1.2.2

Data Representation

Responsibility Assignment Matrix (RAM). An example of a matrix-based chart is a responsibility assignment matrix (RAM) that shows the project resources assigned to each work package. It is used to illustrate the connections between work packages or activities and project team members. On larger projects, RAMs can be developed at various levels. For example, a high-level RAM can define the responsibilities of a project team, group, or unit within each component of the WBS. Lower-level RAMs are used within the group to designate roles, responsibilities, and levels of authority for specific activities. The matrix format shows all activities associated with one person and all people associated with one activity. This also ensures that there is only one person accountable for any one task to avoid confusion about who is ultimately in charge or has authority for the work. One example of a RAM is a RACI (responsible, accountable, consult, and inform) chart, shown in Figure 9-4. The sample chart shows the work to be done in the left column as activities. The assigned resources can be shown as individuals or groups. The project manager can select other options, such as "lead" and "resource" designations, as appropriate for the project. A RACI chart is a useful tool to use to ensure clear assignment of roles and responsibilities when the team consists of internal and external resources.

147. Answer: D.

PMBOK® Guide, pages 318–319, Section 9.1.3

> **Plan Resource Management: Outputs**
> **.1 Resource Management Plan**
> The resource management plan is the component of
> the project management plan that provides guidance
> on how project resources should be categorized,
> allocated, managed, and released. It may be divided
> between the team management plan and physical
> resource management plan according to the specifics
> of the project.
>
> The resource management plan may include, but is not
> limited to the following:
> - **Identification of resources.** Methods for
>   identifying and quantifying team and physical
>   resources needed.
> - **Acquiring resources.** Guidance on how to acquire
>   team and physical resources for the project.
> - **Roles and responsibilities...**

148. Answer: C.

PMBOK® Guide, pages 328–329, Section 9.3

> **Acquire Resources**
> Acquire Resources is the process of obtaining team
> members, facilities, equipment, materials, supplies, and
> other resources necessary to complete project work.
> The key benefit of this process is that it outlines and
> guides the selection of resources and assigns them to their
> respective activities. This process is performed periodically
> throughout the project as needed. The resources needed
> for the project can be internal or external to the project-
> performing organization. Internal resources are acquired
> (assigned) from functional or resource managers. External
> resources are acquired through the procurement processes.
>
> The project management team may or may not have
> direct control over resource selection because of
> collective bargaining agreements, use of subcontractor
> personnel, a matrix project environment, internal or
> external reporting relationships, or other reasons.

149. Answer: B.
PMBOK® Guide, page 328, Section 9.3; and page 331, Section 9.3.1.3

Acquire Resources
Acquire Resources is the process of obtaining team members, facilities, equipment, materials, supplies, and other resources necessary to complete project work. The key benefit of this process is that it outlines and guides the selection of resources and assigns them to their respective activities. This process is performed periodically throughout the project as needed.

Enterprise Environmental Factors
The enterprise environmental factors that can influence the Acquire Resources process include, but are not limited to:
- Existing information on organizational resources, including availability, competence levels, and prior experience for team resources and resource costs;
- Marketplace conditions;
- Organizational structure; and
- Geographic locations.

150. Answer: C.
PMBOK® Guide, page 318, Section 9.1.3.1

Resource Management Plan
The resource management plan is the component of the project management plan that provides guidance on how project resources should be categorized, allocated, managed, and released. It may be divided between the team management plan and physical resource management plan according to the specifics of the project.

151. Answer: D.
PMBOK® Guide, page 341, Section 9.4.2.5

Recognition and Rewards
Part of the team development process involves recognizing and rewarding desirable behavior. The original plan for rewarding people is developed during the Plan Resource Management process. Rewards will be effective only if they satisfy a need that is valued by that individual. Reward decisions are made, formally or informally, during the process of managing the project team. Cultural differences should be considered when determining recognition and rewards. People are motivated if they feel they are valued in the organization and this value is demonstrated by the rewards given to them. Generally, money is viewed as a tangible aspect of any reward system, but intangible rewards could be equally or even more effective. Most project team members are motivated by an opportunity to grow, accomplish, be appreciated, and apply their professional skills to meet new challenges. A good strategy for project managers is to give the team recognition throughout the life cycle of the project rather than waiting until the project is completed.

152. Answer: B.
PMBOK® Guide, Figure 9-8; and pages 332–334, Section 9.3.2

Acquire Resources: Tools and Techniques
.1 Decision making
.2 Interpersonal and team skills
.3 Pre-assignment
.4 Virtual teams

153. Answer: C.

PMBOK® Guide, page 348, Section 9.5.2.1

Interpersonal and Team Skills

Interpersonal and team skills that can be used for this process include, but are not limited to:

Conflict management. Conflict is inevitable in a project environment. Sources of conflict include scarce resources, scheduling priorities, and personal work styles. Team ground rules, group norms, and solid project management practices, such as communication planning and role definition, reduce the amount of conflict. Successful conflict management results in greater productivity and positive working relationships. When managed properly, differences of opinion can lead to increased creativity and better decision making. If the differences become a negative factor, project team members are initially responsible for their resolution. If conflict escalates, the project manager should help facilitate a satisfactory resolution. Conflict should be addressed early and usually in private, using a direct, collaborative approach. If disruptive conflict continues, formal procedures may be used, including disciplinary actions. The success of project managers in managing their project teams often depends on their ability to resolve conflict. Different project managers may use different conflict resolution methods.

Factors that influence conflict resolution methods include:
- Importance and intensity of the conflict,
- Time pressure for resolving the conflict,
- Relative power of the people involved in the conflict,
- Importance of maintaining a good relationship, and
- Motivation to resolve conflict on a long-term or short-term basis.

154. Answer: B.

PMBOK® Guide, page 341, Section 9.4.2.4

Interpersonal and Team Skills

Team building. Team building is conducting activities that enhance the team's social relations and build a collaborative and cooperative working environment. Team building activities can vary from a five-minute agenda item in a status review meeting to an offsite, professionally facilitated event designed to improve interpersonal relationships. The objective of team-building activities is to help individual team members work together effectively. Team-building strategies are particularly valuable when team members operate from remote locations without the benefit of face-to-face contact. Informal communication and activities can help in building trust and establishing good working relationships. While team building is essential during the initial stages of a project, it should be a continuous process. Changes in a project environment are inevitable, and to manage them effectively, a continuous or renewed team-building effort may be applied. The project manager should continually monitor team functionality and performance to determine if any actions are needed to prevent or correct various team problems.

155. Answer: C.

PMBOK® Guide, page 342, Section 9.4.2.6

Training
Training includes all activities designed to enhance the competencies of the project team members. Training can be formal or informal. Examples of training methods include classroom, online, computer-based, on-the-job training from another project team member, mentoring, and coaching. If project team members lack the necessary management or technical skills, such skills can be developed as part of the project work. Scheduled training takes place as stated in the resource management plan. Unplanned training takes place as a result of observation, conversation, and project performance appraisals conducted during management of the project team. Training costs could be included in the project budget or supported by the performing organization if the added skills may be useful for future projects. It may be performed by in-house or by external trainers.

156. Answer: C.

PMBOK® Guide, page 343, Section 9.4.3.1

Team Performance Assessments

As project team development efforts such as training, team building, and colocation are implemented, the project management team makes formal or informal assessments of the project team's effectiveness. Effective team development strategies and activities are expected to increase the team's performance, which increases the likelihood of meeting project objectives. The evaluation of a team's effectiveness may include indicators such as:

- Improvements in skills that allow individuals to perform assignments more effectively;
- Improvements in competencies that help team members perform better as a team;
- Reduced staff turnover rate; and
- Increased team cohesiveness, where team members share information and experiences openly and help one another improve the overall project performance. As a result of conducting an evaluation of the team's overall performance, the project management team can identify the specific training, coaching, mentoring, assistance, or changes required to improve the team's performance. This should also include identifying the appropriate or required resources necessary to achieve and implement the improvements identified in the assessment.

157. Answer: C.
PMBOK® Guide, pages 348–349, Section 9.5.2.1

Interpersonal and Team Skills
There are five general techniques for resolving conflict, each of which has its place and use:
- **Withdraw/avoid.** Retreating from an actual or potential conflict situation; postponing the issue to be better prepared or to be resolved by others.
- **Smooth/accommodate.** Emphasizing areas of agreement rather than areas of difference; conceding one's position to the needs of others to maintain harmony and relationships.
- **Compromise/reconcile.** Searching for solutions that bring some degree of satisfaction to all parties in order to temporarily or partially resolve the conflict. This approach occasionally results in a lose–lose situation.
- **Force/direct.** Pushing one's viewpoint at the expense of others; offering only win–lose solutions, usually enforced through a power position to resolve an emergency. This approach often results in a win–lose situation.
- **Collaborate/problem solve.** Incorporating multiple viewpoints and insights from differing perspectives; requires a cooperative attitude and open dialogue that typically leads to consensus and commitment. This approach can result in a win–win situation.

158. Answer: A.
PMBOK® Guide, page 345, Section 9.5

Manage Team
Manage Team is the process of tracking team member performance, providing feedback, resolving issues, and managing team changes to optimize project performance. The key benefit of this process is that it influences team behavior, manages conflict, and resolves issues. This process is performed throughout the project.

159. Answer: B.
PMBOK® Guide, page 338, Section 9.4

Develop Team
One of the models used to describe team development
is the Tuckman ladder [19, 20], which includes five
stages of development that teams may go through.
Although it is common for these stages to occur in
order, it is not uncommon for a team to get stuck in a
particular stage or regress to an earlier stage. Projects
with team members who worked together in the past
might skip a stage.

- **Forming.** This phase is where the team members
  meet and learn about the project and their formal
  roles and responsibilities. Team members tend to be
  independent and not as open in this phase.
- **Storming.** During this phase, the team begins to
  address the project work, technical decisions, and
  the project management approach. If team members
  are not collaborative or open to differing ideas
  and perspectives, the environment can become
  counterproductive.
- **Norming.** In this phase, team members begin to
  work together and adjust their work habits and
  behaviors to support the team. The team members
  learn to trust one another.
- **Performing.** Teams that reach the performing
  stage function as a well-organized unit. They are
  interdependent and work through issues smoothly
  and effectively.
- **Adjourning.** In this phase, the team completes the
  work and moves on from the project. This typically
  occurs when staff is released from the project
  as deliverables are completed or as part of the
  Close Project or Phase process.

160. Answer: C.
PMBOK® Guide, pages 322–324, Section 9.2.1

Estimate Activity Resources: Inputs
.1 Project management plan
.2 Project documents
.3 Enterprise environmental factors
.4 Organizational process assets

161. Answer: C.
PMBOK® Guide, page 325, Section 9.2.3.1

Resource Requirements
Resource requirements identify the types and quantities of resources required for each work package or activity in a work package and can be aggregated to determine the estimated resources for each work package, each WBS branch, and the project as a whole. The amount of detail and the level of specificity of the resource requirement descriptions can vary by application area. The resource requirements' documentation can include assumptions that were made in determining which types of resources are applied, their availability, and what quantities are needed.

162. Answer: B.

PMBOK® Guide, page 341, Section 9.4.2.4

Team Building
Team building is conducting activities that enhance the team's social relations and build a collaborative and cooperative working environment. Team-building activities can vary from a five-minute agenda item in a status review meeting to an offsite, professionally facilitated event designed to improve interpersonal relationships. The objective of team-building activities is to help individual team members work together effectively. Team-building strategies are particularly valuable when team members operate from remote locations without the benefit of face-face contact. Informal communication and activities can help in building trust and establishing good working relationships. While team building is essential during the initial stages of a project, it should be a continuous process. Changes in a project environment are inevitable, and to manage them effectively, a continuous or renewed team-building effort may be applied. The project manager should continually monitor team functionality and performance to determine if any actions are needed to prevent or correct various team problems.

163. Answer: C.

PMBOK® Guide, page 341, Section 9.4.2.4

Motivation is providing a reason for someone to act. Teams are motivated by empowering them to participate in decision making and encouraging them to work independently.

Project Communications Management
(Section 10 of the *PMBOK® Guide*)

164. Answer: A.
PMBOK® Guide, pages 359–360, Introduction; and page 360, Figure 10-1

Project Communications Management
Figure 10-1 provides an overview of the Project Communications Management processes, which are as follows:

10.1 Plan Communications Management—The process of developing an appropriate approach and plan for project communications based on stakeholders' information needs and requirements, and available organizational assets.

10.2 Manage Communications—The process of creating, collecting, distributing, storing, retrieving, and the ultimate disposition of project information in accordance with the communications management plan.

10.3 Monitor Communications—The process of monitoring and controlling communications throughout the entire project life cycle to ensure that the information needs of the project stakeholders are met.

165. Answer: A.
PMBOK® Guide, pages 366–367, Section 10.1; and page 366, Figure 10-2

The Plan Communications Management inputs are as follows:
Project charter
Project management plan
- Resource management plan
- Stakeholder engagement plan

Project documents
- Requirements documentation
- Stakeholder register

Enterprise environmental factors
Organizational process assets

166. Answer: D.
PMBOK® Guide, pages 368–370, Section 10.1.1.2, Section 4.2.3.1

Communications Management Plan

The communications management plan is a component of the project management plan that describes how project communications will be planned, structured, monitored, and controlled. The plan contains the following information:

- Stakeholder communication requirements;
- Information to be communicated, including language, format, content, and level of detail;
- Reason for the distribution of that information;
- Time frame and frequency for the distribution of required information and receipt of acknowledgment or response, if applicable;
- Person responsible for communicating the information;
- Person responsible for authorizing release of confidential information;
- Person or groups who will receive the information;
- Methods or technologies used to convey the information, such as memos, email, and/or press releases;
- Resources allocated for communication activities, including time and budget;
- Escalation process identifying time frames and the management chain (names) for escalation of issues that cannot be resolved at a lower staff level;
- Method for updating and refining the communications management plan as the project progresses and develops;
- Glossary of common terminology;
- Flow charts of the information flow in the project, workflows with possible sequence of authorization, list of reports, and meeting plans, etc.; and
- Communication constraints usually derived from a specific legislation or regulation, technology, and organizational policies, etc.

The communications management plan can also include guidelines and templates for project status meetings, project team meetings, e-meetings, and email messages. The use of a project website and project management software can also be included if these are to be used in the project.

167. Answer: A.
PMBOK® Guide, page 385, Section 10.2.2.4

Project Management Information Systems (PMIS)
Project management information systems can ensure that stakeholders can easily retrieve the information they need in a timely way. Project information is managed and distributed using a variety of tools, including:
- Electronic project management tools. Project management software, meeting and virtual office support software, web interfaces, specialized project portals and dashboards, and collaborative work management tools.
- Electronic communications management. Email, fax, and voicemail; audio, video, and web conferencing; and websites and web publishing.
- Social media management. Websites and web publishing; and blogs and applications, which offer the opportunity to engage with stakeholders and form online communities.

168. Answer: C.
PMBOK® Guide, pages 370–371, Section 10.1.2.3

Communication Technology
The methods used to transfer information among project stakeholders may vary significantly…

Factors that can affect the choice of communication technology include:
- **Urgency of the need for information…**
- **Availability of technology…**
- **Ease of use…**
- **Project environment…**
- **Sensitivity and confidentiality of the information…**

169. Answer: B.

PMBOK® Guide, pages 371–373, Section 10.1.2.4; and Figure 10-4

Communication Models

The communication models used to facilitate communications and the exchange of information may vary from project to project and also within different stages of the same project. A basic communication model, shown in Figure 10-4, consists of two parties, defined as the sender and receiver. Medium is the technology medium and includes the mode of communication, while noise includes any interference or barriers that might compromise the delivery of the message.

The components of the basic communications model need to be considered when project communications are discussed. As part of the communications process, the sender is responsible for the transmission of the message, ensuring that the information being communicated is clear and complete, and confirming the communication is correctly understood. The receiver is responsible for ensuring that the information is received in its entirety, understood correctly, and acknowledged or responded to appropriately.

PMBOK® Guide, pages 371–373, Section 10.1.2.4; and Figure 10-4

Communication Models

The components of the basic communication model need to be considered when project communications are discussed. As part of the communications process, the sender is responsible for the transmission of the message, ensuring that the information being communicated is clear and complete, and confirming the communication is correctly understood.

The receiver is responsible for ensuring that the information is received in its entirety, understood correctly, and acknowledged or responded to appropriately.

Listening is an important part of communication. Listening techniques, both active and passive, give the user insight to problem areas, negotiation and conflict management strategies, decision making, and problem resolution.

171. Answer: D.

PMBOK® Guide, pages 369–370, Section 10.1.2.2

Communication Requirements Analysis

Analysis of communication requirements determines the information needs of the project stakeholders. These requirements are defined by combining the type and format of information needed with an analysis of the value of that information.

Sources of information typically used to identify and define project communication requirements include, but are not limited to:

- Stakeholder information and communication requirements from within the stakeholder register and stakeholder engagement plan;
- Number of potential communication channels or paths, including one-to-one, one-to-many, and many-to-many communications;
- Organizational charts;
- Project organization and stakeholder responsibilities, relationships, and interdependencies;
- Development approach;
- Disciplines, departments, and specialties involved in the project;
- Logistics of how many persons will be involved with the project and at which locations;
- Internal information needs (e.g., when communicating within organizations);
- External information needs (e.g., when communicating with the media, public, or contractors); and
- Legal requirements.

172. Answer: C.

PMBOK® Guide, pages 359–362, Introduction

Project Communications Management

Communications activities have many dimensions, including but not limited to the following:

- **Internal.** Focus on stakeholders within the project and within the organization.
- **External.** Focus on external stakeholders such as customers, vendors, other projects, organizations, government, the public, and environmental advocates.
- **Formal.** Reports, formal meetings (both regular and ad hoc), meeting agendas and minutes, stakeholder briefings, and presentations.
- **Informal.** General communications activities using emails, social media, websites, and informal ad hoc discussions.
- **Hierarchical focus.** The position of the stakeholder or group with respect to the project team will affect the format and content of the message, in the following ways:
  - **Upward.** Senior management stakeholders.
  - **Downward.** The team and others who will contribute to the work of the project.
  - **Horizontal.** Peers of the project manager or team.
- **Official.** Annual reports; reports to regulators or government bodies.
- **Unofficial.** Communications that focus on establishing and maintaining the profile and recognition of the project and building strong relationships between the project team and its stakeholders using flexible, and often informal, means.
- **Written and oral.** Verbal (words and voice inflections) and nonverbal (body language and actions), social media and websites, media releases.

173. Answer: C.

PMBOK® Guide, page 385, Section 10.2.2.4

> **Project Management Information System (PMIS)**
> Described in Section 4.3.2.2, project management information systems can ensure that stakeholders can easily retrieve the information they need in a timely way. Project information is managed and distributed using a variety of tools, including the following:
> - **Electronic project management tools.** Project management software, meeting and virtual office support software, web interfaces, specialized project portals and dashboards, and collaborative work management tools.
> - **Electronic communications management.** Email, fax, and voicemail; audio, video, and web conferencing; and websites and web publishing.
> - **Social media management.** Websites and web publishing; and blogs and applications, which offer the opportunity to engage with stakeholders and form online communities.

174. Answer: D.

PMBOK® Guide, pages 379–380, Section 10.2, Figure 10-5

Manage Communications

Techniques and considerations for effective communications management include, but are not limited to, the following:

- Communications technology
- Communication skills
  - Communication competence
  - Feedback
  - Nonverbal
  - Presentations
- Project management information systems (PMIS)
- Project reporting
- Interpersonal and team skills
  - Active listening
  - Conflict management
  - Cultural awareness
  - Meeting management
  - Networking
  - Political awareness
- Meetings

175. Answer: B.

PMBOK® Guide, page 388, Section 10.3, Figure 10-7

Monitor Communications

Monitor Communications is the process of monitoring and controlling communications throughout the entire project life cycle to ensure that the information needs of the project stakeholders are met. The key benefit of this process is that it ensures optimal information flow among all communication participants, at any moment in time.

Project Risk Management
(Section 11 of the *PMBOK® Guide*)

176. Answer: D.
PMBOK® Guide, pages 395–396, Introduction; and page 396, Figure 11-1

Project Risk Management Processes
Project Risk Management includes the processes of conducting risk management planning, identification, analysis, response planning, and controlling risk on a project. The objectives of project risk management are to increase the likelihood and impact of positive events, and decrease the likelihood and impact of negative events in the project.

Figure 11-1 provides an overview of the Project Risk Management processes, which are as follows:

11.1 Plan Risk Management—The process of defining how to conduct risk management activities for a project.

11.2 Identify Risks—The process of determining which risks may affect the project and documenting their characteristics.

11.3 Perform Qualitative Risk Analysis—The process of prioritizing risks for further analysis or action by assessing and combining their probability of occurrence and impact.

11.4 Perform Quantitative Risk Analysis—The process of numerically analyzing the effect of identified risks on overall project objectives.

11.5 Plan Risk Responses—The process of developing options and actions to enhance opportunities and to reduce threats to project objectives.

11.6 Implement Risk Responses—The process of implementing predefined risk responses as risks occur on the project.

11.7 Monitor Risks—The process of implementing risk response plans, tracking identified risks, monitoring residual risks, identifying new risks, and evaluating risk process effectiveness throughout the project.

177. Answer: A.

PMBOK® Guide, pages 442–443, Section 11.5.2.4

Strategies for Threats

Three strategies, which typically deal with threats or risks that may have negative impacts on project objectives if they occur, are: avoid, transfer, and mitigate. The fourth strategy, accept, can be used for negative risks or threats as well as positive risks or opportunities. Each of these risk response strategies has varied and unique influence on the risk condition. These strategies should be chosen to match the risk's probability and impact on the project's overall objectives. Avoidance and mitigation strategies are usually good strategies for critical risks with high impact, while transference and acceptance are usually good strategies for threats that are less critical and with low overall impact.

178. Answer: D.

PMBOK® Guide, pages 442–443, Section 11.5.2.4

Strategies for Threats

Transfer involves shifting ownership of a threat to a third party to manage the risk and bear the impact if the threat occurs. Risk transfer often involves payment of a risk premium to the party taking on the threat. Transfer can be achieved by a range of actions, which include, but are not limited to, the use of insurance, performance bonds, warranties, guarantees, etc. Agreements may be used to transfer ownership and liability for specified risks to another party.

Risk transference is a risk response strategy whereby the project team shifts the impact of a threat to a third party, together with ownership of the response. Transferring the risk simply gives another party responsibility for its management—it does not eliminate it. Transferring does not mean disowning the risk by transferring it to a later project or another person without his or her knowledge or agreement.

Risk transference nearly always involves payment of a risk premium to the party taking on the risk. Transferring liability for risk is most effective in dealing with financial risk exposure. Transference tools can be quite diverse and include, but are not limited to, the use of insurance, performance bonds, warranties, guarantees, etc.

Contracts or agreements may be used to transfer liability for specified risks to another party. For example, when a buyer has capabilities that the seller does not possess, it may be prudent to transfer some work and its concurrent risk contractually back to the buyer. In many cases, use of a cost-plus contract may transfer the cost risk to the buyer, while a fixed-price contract may transfer risk to the seller.

179. Answer: C.

PMBOK® Guide, pages 442–443, Section 11.5.2.4

Strategies for Threats

Risk acceptance acknowledges the existence of a threat, but no proactive action is taken. This strategy may be appropriate for low-priority threats, and it may also be adopted where it is not possible or cost-effective to address a threat in any other way. Acceptance can be either active or passive. The most common active acceptance strategy is to establish a contingency reserve, including amounts of time, money, or resources to handle the threat if it occurs. Passive acceptance involves no proactive action apart from periodic review of the threat to ensure that it does not change significantly.

Risk acceptance is a risk response strategy whereby the project team decides to acknowledge the risk and not take any action unless the risk occurs. This strategy is adopted where it is not possible or cost-effective to address a specific risk in any other way. This strategy indicates that the project team has decided not to change the project management plan to deal with a risk, or is unable to identify any other suitable response strategy. This strategy can be either passive or active.

Passive acceptance requires no action except to document the strategy, leaving the project team to deal with the risks as they occur, and to periodically review the threat to ensure that it does not change significantly. The most common active acceptance strategy is to establish a contingency reserve, including amounts of time, money, or resources to handle the risks.

180. Answer: A.

PMBOK® Guide, pages 417–418, Section 11.2.3, Figure 11-6

Identify Risks: Outputs
.1 Risk Register

The primary output from Identify Risks is the initial entry into the risk register. The risk register is a document in which the results of risk analysis and risk response planning are recorded. It contains the outcomes of the other risk management processes as they are conducted, resulting in an increase in the level and type of information contained in the risk register over time. The preparation of the risk register begins in the Identify Risks process with the following information, and then becomes available to other project management and risk management processes:

- **List of identified risks...**
- **List of potential responses...**

181. Answer: A.

PMBOK® Guide, page 414, Section 11.2.2.2

Data Gathering

Checklists. A checklist is a list of items, actions, or points to be considered. It is often used as a reminder. Risk checklists are developed based on historical information and knowledge that has been accumulated from similar projects and from other sources of information. They are an effective way to capture lessons learned from similar completed projects, listing specific individual project risks that have occurred previously and that may be relevant to this project. The organization may maintain a risk checklist based on its own completed projects or may use generic risk checklists from the industry. While a checklist may be quick and simple to use, it is impossible to build an exhaustive one, and care should be taken to ensure that the checklist is not used to avoid the effort of proper risk identification. The project team should also explore items that do not appear on the checklist. Additionally, the checklist should be reviewed from time to time to update new information as well as remove or archive obsolete information.

182. Answer: C.

PMBOK® Guide, pages 411–412, Section 11.2.1; and Figure 11-6

The Identify Risks process has the following inputs:
- Project management plan
  - Requirements management plan
  - Schedule management plan
  - Cost management plan
  - Resource management plan
  - Risk management plan
  - Quality management plan
  - Scope baseline
  - Schedule baseline
  - Cost baseline
- Project documents
  - Assumption log
  - Cost estimates
  - Duration estimates
  - Issue log
  - Lessons learned register
  - Requirements documentation
  - Resource requirements
  - Stakeholder register
- Agreements
- Procurement documentation
- Enterprise environmental factors
- Organizational process assets

183. Answer: B.

PMBOK® Guide, pages 437–438, Section 11.5.3; and Figure 11-1(

The Plan Risk Responses process has the following outputs:
- Change requests
- Project management plan updates
  - Schedule management plan
  - Cost management plan
  - Quality management plan
  - Resource management plan
  - Procurement management plan
  - Scope baseline
  - Schedule baseline
  - Cost baseline
- Project documents updates
  - Assumption log
  - Cost forecasts
  - Lessons learned register
  - Project schedule
  - Risk register

184. Answer: D.

PMBOK® Guide, pages 428–432, Section 11.4.2; and page 428, Figure 11-11

The Perform Quantitative Risk Analysis process has the following tools and techniques:
- Expert judgment
- Data gathering
  - Interviews
- Interpersonal and team skills
  - Facilitation
- Representations of uncertainty
- Data analysis
  - Simulations
  - Sensitivity analysis
  - Decision tree analysis
  - Influence diagrams

185. Answer: A.

PMBOK® Guide, page 436, Section 11.4.3; and page 428, Figure 11-11

The Perform Quantitative Risk Analysis process has the following outputs:
- Project documents updates
  - Risk report

186. Answer: D.

PMBOK® Guide, page 407-408, Table 11-1; page 423, and Section 11.3.2

Definitions of Risk Probability and Impact

Definitions of risk probability and impact levels are specific to the project context and reflect the risk appetite and thresholds of the organization and key stakeholders. The project may generate specific definitions of probability and impact levels or it may start with general definitions provided by the organization. The number of levels reflects the degree of detail required for the Project Risk Management process, with more levels used for a more detailed risk approach (typically five levels), and fewer for a simple process (usually three). Table 11-1 provides an example of definitions of probability and impacts against three project objectives.

Probability and Impact Matrix

Opportunities and threats are represented in a common probability and impact matrix using positive definitions of impact for opportunities and negative impact definitions for threats. Descriptive terms (such as very high, high, medium, low, and very low) or numeric values can be used for probability and impact. Where numeric values are used, these can be multiplied to give a probability-impact score for each risk, which allows the relative priority of individual risks to be evaluated within each priority level. An example probability and impact matrix is presented in Figure 11-5, which also shows a possible numeric risk scoring scheme.

Risk Probability and Impact Assessment

Risk probability assessment considers the likelihood that a specific risk will occur. Risk impact assessment considers the potential effect on one or more project objectives such as schedule, cost, quality, or performance. Impacts will be negative for threats and positive for opportunities. . .

87. Answer: B.

PMBOK® Guide, page 457, Section 11.7.3; and page 453, Figure 11-20

> **The Monitor Risks process has the following outputs:**
> .1 Work Performance Information
> .2 Change Requests
> .3 Project Management Plan Updates
> .4 Project Document Updates
> .5 Organizational Process Assets Updates

88. Answer: A.

PMBOK® Guide, pages 425–426, Section 11.3.2.6; and Figure 11-5

> **Probability and Impact Matrix**
> Described in Section 11.3.2.6, prioritization rules may be specified by the organization in advance of the project and be included in organizational process assets, or they may be tailored to the specific project.
>
> Opportunities and threats are represented in a common probability and impact matrix using positive definitions of impact for opportunities and negative impact definitions for threats. Descriptive terms (such as *very high*, *high*, *medium*, *low*, and *very low*) or numeric values can be used for probability and impact. Where numeric values are used, these can be multiplied to give a probability-impact score for each risk, which allows the relative priority of individual risks to be evaluated within each priority level.
>
> An example probability and impact matrix is presented in Figure 11-5, which also shows a possible numeric risk-scoring scheme.

189. Answer: B.

PMBOK® Guide, pages 433–434, Section 11.4.2.5; and Figure 11-14

Sensitivity Analysis

Sensitivity analysis (also called a tornado diagram) helps determine which individual project risks or other sources of uncertainty have the most potential impact on project outcomes. It correlates variations in project outcomes with variations in elements of the quantitative risk analysis model. One typical display of sensitivity analysis is the tornado diagram, which presents the calculated correlation coefficient for each element of the quantitative risk analysis model that can influence the project outcome. This can include individual project risks, project activities with high degrees of variability, or specific sources of ambiguity. Items are ordered by descending strength of correlation, giving the typical tornado appearance. An example tornado diagram is shown in Figure 11-14

190. Answer: C.
PMBOK® Guide, page 432, Section 11.4.2.4

Probability distributions. Continuous probability distributions, which are used extensively in modeling and simulation, represent the uncertainty in values such as durations of schedule activities and costs of project components. Discrete distributions can be used to represent uncertain events, such as the outcome of a test or a possible scenario in a decision tree.

Expected monetary value analysis. Expected monetary value (EMV) analysis is a statistical concept that calculates the average outcome when the future includes scenarios that may or may not happen (i.e., analysis under uncertainty). The EMV of opportunities is generally expressed as positive values, while the EMV of threats is expressed as negative values. EMV requires a risk-neutral assumption—neither risk-averse nor risk-seeking. EMV for a project is calculated by multiplying the value of each possible outcome by its probability of occurrence and adding the products together. A common use of this type of analysis is a decision tree analysis (Figure 11-15).

Plan Risk Responses: Tools and Techniques
Several risk response strategies are available. The strategy or mix of strategies most likely to be effective should be selected for each risk. Risk analysis tools, such as decision tree analysis (Section 11.4.2.5), can be used to choose the most appropriate responses.

Decision tree analysis is a diagramming and calculation technique for evaluating the implications of a chain of multiple options in the presence of uncertainty.

191. Answer: C.

PMBOK® Guide, page 405, Section 11.1.3.1

Risk Management Plan

The risk management plan is a component of the project management plan that describes how risk management activities will be structured and performed. The risk management plan may include some or all of the following elements:

- **Risk strategy.** Describes the general approach to managing risk on the project. .
- **Methodology.** Defines the specific approaches, tools, and data sources that will be used to perform risk management on the project.
- **Roles and responsibilities.** Defines the lead, support, and risk management team members for each type of activity described in the risk management plan, and clarifies their responsibilities.
- **Funding.** Identifies the funds needed to perform activities related to Project Risk Management. Establishes protocols for the application of contingency and management reserves.
- **Timing.** Defines when and how often the Project Risk Management processes will be performed throughout the project life cycle, and establishes risk management activities for inclusion into the project schedule.
- **Risk categories.** Provide a means for grouping individual project risks. A common way to structure risk categories is with a risk breakdown structure (RBS), which is a hierarchical representation of potential sources of risk (see the example in Figure 11-4). An RBS helps the project team consider the full range of sources from which individual project risks may arise. This can be useful when identifying risks or when categorizing identified risks. The organization may have a generic RBS to be used for all projects, or there may be several RBS frameworks for different types of projects, or the project may develop a tailored RBS. Where an RBS is not used, an organization may use a custom risk categorization framework, which may take the form of a simple list of categories or a structure based on project objectives.

192. Answer: C.

PMBOK® Guide, page 419, Section 11.3

Perform Qualitative Risk Analysis

Perform Qualitative Risk Analysis is the process of prioritizing individual project risks for further analysis or action by assessing their probability of occurrence and impact as well as other characteristics. The key benefit of this process is that it focuses efforts on high-priority risks. This process is performed throughout the project. The inputs, tools and techniques, and outputs of the process are depicted in Figure 11-8. Figure 11-9 depicts the data flow diagram for the process.

193. Answer: A.

PMBOK® Guide, page 453, Section 11.7

Monitor Risks is the process of monitoring the implementation of agreed-upon risk response plans, tracking identified risks, identifying and analyzing new risks, and evaluating risk process effectiveness throughout the project. The key benefit of this process is that it enables project decisions to be based on current information about overall project risk exposure and individual project risks. This process is performed throughout the project. The inputs, tools and techniques, and outputs of the process are depicted in Figure 11-20. Figure 11-21 depicts the data flow diagram for the process.

194. Answer: B.
PMBOK® Guide, page 415, Section 11.2.2.3

Data Analysis
SWOT analysis examines the project from each of the strengths, weaknesses, opportunities, and threats perspectives. For risk identification, it is used to increase the breadth of identified risks by including internally generated risks. The technique starts with the identification of strengths and weaknesses of the organization, focusing on either the project, organization, or the business area in general. SWOT analysis then identifies any opportunities for the project that may arise from strengths, and any threats resulting from weaknesses. The analysis also examines the degree to which organizational strengths may offset threats and determines if weaknesses might hinder opportunities.

195. Answer: D.
PMBOK® Guide, page 450, Section 11.6.1

The Implement Risk Responses process has the following inputs:
- Project management plan
  - Risk management plan
- Project documents
  - Lessons learned register
  - Risk register
  - Risk report
- Organizational process assets

Project Procurement Management
(Section 12 of the *PMBOK® Guide*)

196. Answer: C.
PMBOK® Guide, pages 466–467, Section 12.1; and Figure 12-2

The Plan Procurement Management process has the following inputs:
- Project charter
- Business documents
  - Business case
  - Benefits management plan
- Project management plan
  - Scope management plan
  - Quality management plan
  - Resource management plan
  - Scope baseline
- Project documents
  - Milestone list
  - Project team assignments
  - Requirements documentation
  - Requirements traceability matrix
  - Resource requirements
  - Risk register
  - Stakeholder register
- Enterprise environmental factors
- Organizational process assets

197. Answer: A.
PMBOK® Guide, page 477, Section 12.1.3.3

Procurement Documentation
Procurement documentation provides a written record used in reaching the legal agreement, and may include older documents predating the current project. Procurement documentation can include:
- **Bid documents.** Described in Section 12.1.3.3, procurement documents include the RFI, RFP, RFQ, or other documents sent to sellers so they can develop a bid response.

12.2.1.4 Seller Proposals
Seller proposals, prepared in response to a procurement document package, form the basic information that will be used by an evaluation body to select one or more successful bidders (sellers). If the seller is going to submit a price proposal, good practice is to require that it be separate from the technical proposal. The evaluation body reviews each submitted proposal according to the source selection criteria and selects the seller that can best satisfy the buying organization's requirements.

198. Answer: D.

PMBOK® Guide, page 485, Section 12.2.1.3

Procurement Documentation

Procurement documentation provides a written record used in reaching the legal agreement, and may include older documents predating the current project. Procurement documentation can include the following:

- **Bid documents.** Described in Section 12.1.3.3, procurement documents include the RFI, RFP, RFQ, or other documents sent to sellers so they can develop a bid response.
- **Procurement statement of work.** Described in Section 12.1.3.4, the procurement statement of work (SOW) provides sellers with a clearly stated set of goals, requirements, and outcomes from which they can provide a quantifiable response.
- **Independent cost estimates.** Described in Section 12.1.3.7, independent cost estimates are developed either internally or by using external resources and provide a reasonableness check against the proposals submitted by bidders.
- **Source selection criteria.** Described in Section 12.1.3.5, these criteria describe how bidder proposals will be evaluated, including evaluation criteria and weights. For risk mitigation, the buyer may decide to sign agreements with more than one seller to mitigate damage caused by a single seller having problems that impact the overall project.

199. Answer: C.
PMBOK® Guide, page 496, Section 12.3.1.5

Approved Change Requests
Approved change requests can include modifications to the terms and conditions of the contract, including the procurement statement of work (SOW), pricing, and descriptions of the products, services, or results to be provided. All procurement-related changes are formally documented in writing and approved before being implemented through the Control Procurements process. In complex programs and projects, change requests may come from sellers involved with the project that can influence other involved sellers. The project should have the capability of identifying, communicating, and resolving changes that impact the work of multiple sellers.

200. Answer: B.
PMBOK® Guide, page 487, Section 12.2.2.2

Advertising
Existing lists of potential sellers often can be expanded by placing advertisements in general circulation publications, such as selected newspapers or in specialty trade publications. Some organizations use online resources to communicate solicitations to the vendor community. Some government jurisdictions require public advertising of certain types of procurement items, and most government jurisdictions require public advertising or online posting of pending government contracts.

201. Answer: A.
PMBOK® Guide, page 492, Section 12.3

Control Procurements
The buyer, usually through its authorized procurement administrator, provides the seller with formal written notice that the contract has been completed. Requirements for formal procurement closure are usually defined in the terms and conditions of the contract and are included in the procurement management plan.

. . .

Deliverable acceptance. Documentation of formal acceptance of seller-provided deliverables may be required to be retained by the organization. The Close Procurement process ensures that this documentation requirement is satisfied. Requirements for formal deliverable acceptance and how to address nonconforming deliverables are usually defined in the agreement.

202. Answer: B.
PMBOK® Guide, page 471, Section 12.1.1.6

Organizational Process Assets
Fixed-price contracts. This category of contracts involves setting a fixed total price for a defined product, service, or result to be provided. These contracts should be used when the requirements are well defined and no significant changes to the scope are expected. Types of fixed-price contracts include:

- **Firm fixed price (FFP).** The most commonly used contract type is the FFP. It is favored by most buying organizations because the price for goods is set at the outset and not subject to change unless the scope of work changes.
- **Fixed price incentive fee (FPIF).** This fixed-price arrangement gives the buyer and seller some flexibility in that it allows for deviation from performance, with financial incentives tied to achieving agreed-upon metrics. Typically, such financial incentives are related to cost, schedule, or technical performance of the seller. Under FPIF contracts, a price ceiling is set, and all costs above the price ceiling are the responsibility of the seller.
- **Fixed price with economic price adjustments (FPEPA).** This type is used whenever the seller's performance period spans a considerable period of years, or if the payments are made in a different currency. It is a fixed-price contract, but with a special provision allowing for predefined final adjustments to the contract price due to changed conditions, such as inflation changes or cost increases (or decreases) for specific commodities.

203. Answer: D.
PMBOK® Guide, page 498, Section 12.3.2.2

Claims Administration
Contested changes and potential constructive changes
are those requested changes where the buyer and
seller cannot reach an agreement on compensation
for the change or cannot agree that a change has
occurred. These contested changes are called
claims. When they cannot be resolved, they become
disputes, and finally, appeals. Claims are documented,
processed, monitored, and managed throughout the
contract life cycle, usually in accordance with the
terms of the contract. If the parties themselves do
not resolve a claim, it may have to be handled in
accordance with alternative dispute resolution (ADR)
typically following procedures established in the
contract. Settlement of all claims and disputes through
negotiation is the preferred method.

204. Answer: C.
PMBOK® Guide, page 499, Section 12.3.3.4

12.3.3.4 Change Requests
Described in Section 4.3.3.4, change requests to
the project management plan, its subsidiary plans,
and other components such as the cost baseline,
schedule baseline, and procurement management
plan, may result from the Control Procurements
process. Change requests are processed for review
and disposition through the Perform Integrated
Change Control process (Section 4.6). Requested but
unresolved changes can include direction provided
by the buyer or actions taken by the seller, which the
other party considers a constructive change to the
contract. Because any of these constructive changes
may be disputed by one party and can lead to a claim
against the other party, such changes are uniquely
identified and documented by project correspondence.

205. Answer: A.

PMBOK® Guide, page 471, Section 12.1.1.6

Organizational Process Assets

Fixed-price contracts. This category of contracts involves setting a fixed total price for a defined product, service, or result to be provided.
These contracts should be used when the requirements are well defined and no significant changes to the scope are expected. Types of fixed-price contracts include the following:

- **Cost-reimbursable contracts.** This category of contract involves payments (cost reimbursements) to the seller for all legitimate actual costs incurred for completed work, plus a fee representing seller profit. This type should be used if the scope of work is expected to change significantly during the execution of the contract.

- **Time and material contracts (T&M).** Time and material contracts (also called time and means) are a hybrid type of contractual arrangement with aspects of both cost-reimbursable and fixed-price contracts. They are often used for staff augmentation, acquisition of experts, and any outside support when a precise statement of work cannot be quickly prescribed.

206. Answer: B.

PMBOK® Guide, page 477, Section 12.1.3.4

Procurement Statement of Work

The statement of work (SOW) for each procurement is developed from the project scope baseline and defines only that portion of the project scope that is to be included within the related contract. The SOW describes the procurement item in sufficient detail to allow prospective sellers to determine if they are capable of providing the products, services, or results. Sufficient detail can vary based on the nature of the item, the needs of the buyer, or the expected contract form. Information included in a SOW can include specifications, quantity desired, quality levels, performance data, period of performance, work location, and other requirements. The procurement SOW should be clear, complete, and concise. It includes a description of any collateral services required, such as performance reporting or post-project operational support for the procured item. The SOW can be revised as required as it moves through the procurement process until it is incorporated into a signed agreement.

207. Answer: D.

PMBOK® Guide, page 478, Section 12.1.3.5

Source Selection Criteria

In choosing evaluation criteria, the buyer seeks to ensure that the proposal selected will offer the best quality for the services required. The source selection criteria may include, but are not limited to:

- Capability and capacity;
- Product cost and life cycle cost;
- Delivery dates;
- Technical expertise and approach;
- Specific relevant experience;
- Adequacy of the proposed approach and work plan in responding to the SOW;
- Key staff's qualifications, availability, and competence;
- Financial stability of the firm;
- Management experience; and
- Suitability of the knowledge transfer program, including training.

For international projects, evaluation criteria may include "local content" requirements—for example, participation by nationals among proposed key staff.

208. Answer: D.

PMBOK® Guide, pages 482–483, Section 12.2

The Conduct Procurements process has the following tools and techniques:
.1 Expert judgment
.2 Advertising
.3 Bidder conferences
.4 Data analysis
- Proposal evaluation
.5 Negotiation

209. Answer: B.
PMBOK® Guide, page 471, Section 12.1.1.6

Organizational Process Assets
Cost-reimbursable contracts. This category of contract involves payments (cost reimbursements) to the seller for all legitimate actual costs incurred for completed work, plus a fee representing seller profit. This type should be used if the scope of work is expected to change significantly during the execution of the contract.

Variations can include:
- **Cost plus fixed fee (CPFF).** The seller is reimbursed for all allowable costs for performing the contract work and receives a fixed-fee payment calculated as a percentage of the initial estimated project costs. Fee amounts do not change unless the project scope changes.

210. Answer: C.
PMBOK® Guide, page 479, Section 12.1.3.6

Make-or-Buy Decisions
A make-or-buy analysis results in a decision as to whether particular work can best be accomplished by the project team or needs to be purchased from outside sources.

211. Answer: B.
PMBOK® Guide, page 488, Section 12.2.2.5

Interpersonal and Team Skills
Interpersonal and team skills that can be used
for this process include negotiation. Negotiation
is a discussion aimed at reaching an agreement.
Procurement negotiation clarifies the structure, rights,
and obligations of the parties and other terms of the
purchases so that mutual agreement can be reached
prior to signing the contract. Final document language
reflects all agreements reached. Negotiation concludes
with a signed contract document or other formal
agreement that can be executed by both buyer and
seller. The negotiation should be led by a member of
the procurement team that has the authority to sign
contracts. The project manager and other members of
the project management team may be present during
negotiation to provide assistance as needed.

Project Stakeholder Management
(Section 13 of the *PMBOK® Guide*)

212. Answer: B.
PMBOK® Guide, pages 503–504, Section 13

Project Stakeholder Management
Project Stakeholder Management includes the processes required to identify the people, groups, or organizations that could impact or be impacted by the project, to analyze stakeholder expectations and their impact on the project, and to develop appropriate management strategies for effectively engaging stakeholders in project decisions and execution.
The processes support the work of the project team to analyze stakeholder expectations, assess the degree to which they impact or are impacted by the project, and develop strategies to effectively engage stakeholders in support of project decisions and the planning and execution of the work of the project.

213. Answer: B.

PMBOK® Guide, pages 503–504, Section 13

The Project Stakeholder Management processes are as follows:

13.1 Identify Stakeholders—The process of identifying project stakeholders regularly and analyzing and documenting relevant information regarding their interests, involvement, interdependencies, influence, and potential impacts on project success.

13.2 Plan Stakeholder Engagement—The process of developing approaches to involve project stakeholders based on their needs, expectations, interests, and potential impacts on the project.

13.3 Manage Stakeholder Engagement—The process of communicating and working with stakeholders to meet their needs and expectations, address issues, and foster appropriate stakeholder engagement involvement.

13.4 Monitor Stakeholder Engagement—The process of monitoring project stakeholder relationships and tailoring strategies for engaging stakeholders through the modification of engagement strategies and plans.

214. Answer: C.

PMBOK® Guide, page 504, Figure 13-1

Manage Stakeholder Engagement

Manage Stakeholder Engagement is the process of communicating and working with stakeholders to meet their needs and expectations, address issues, and foster appropriate stakeholder involvement. The key benefit of this process is that it allows the project manager to increase support and minimize resistance from stakeholders. This process is performed throughout the project. The inputs, tools and techniques, and outputs of the process are depicted in Figure 13-7. Figure 13-8 depicts the data flow diagram for the process.

215. Answer: C.
PMBOK® Guide, page 516, Section 13.2

Plan Stakeholder Engagement
Plan Stakeholder Engagement is the process of
developing approaches to involve project stakeholders
based on their needs, expectations, interests, and
potential impacts on the project. The key benefit is that
it provides an actionable plan to interact effectively
with stakeholders. This process is performed
periodically throughout the project as needed.
(The *PMBOK® Guide* – Fifth Edition called this process
Plan Stakeholder Management.)

216. Answer: A.
PMBOK® Guide, page 523, Section 13.3

Manage Stakeholder Engagement
Manage Stakeholder Engagement is the process of
communicating and working with stakeholders to meet
their needs and expectations, address issues, and foster
appropriate stakeholder involvement. The key benefit
of this process is that it allows the project manager
to increase support and minimize resistance from
stakeholders. This process is performed throughout the
project. The inputs, tools and techniques, and outputs
of the process are depicted in Figure 13-7. Figure 13-8
depicts the data flow diagram for the process.

217. Answer: D.
PMBOK® Guide, page 530, Section 13.4

> **Monitor Stakeholder Engagement**
> Monitor Stakeholder Engagement is the process of
> monitoring project stakeholder relationships and
> tailoring strategies for engaging stakeholders through
> modification of engagement strategies and plans.
> The key benefit of this process is that it maintains
> or increases the efficiency and effectiveness of
> stakeholder engagement activities as the project
> evolves and its environment changes. This process
> is performed throughout the project. The inputs,
> tools and techniques, and outputs of the process are
> depicted in Figure 13-9. Figure 13-10 depicts the data
> flow diagram for the process.

218. Answer: C.
PMBOK® Guide, page 512, Section 13.1.2.4

> **Data Representation**
> **Power/interest grid, power/influence grid, or
> impact/influence grid.** Each of these techniques
> supports a grouping of stakeholders according to their
> level of authority (power), level of concern about the
> project's outcomes (interest), ability to influence the
> outcomes of the project (influence), or ability to cause
> changes to the project's planning or execution. These
> classification models are useful for small projects
> or for projects with simple relationships between
> stakeholders and the project, or within the stakeholder
> community itself.

219. Answer: D.

PMBOK® Guide, page 514, Section 13.1.3.1

Stakeholder Register

The main output of the Identify Stakeholders process is the stakeholder register. This document contains information about identified stakeholders that includes, but is not limited to, the following:

- **Identification information.** Name, organizational position, location and contact details, and role on the project.
- **Assessment information.** Major requirements, expectations, potential for influencing project outcomes, and the phase of the project life cycle where the stakeholder has the most influence or impact.
- **Stakeholder classification.** Internal/external, impact/influence, power/interest, upward/downward, outward/sideward, or any other classification model chosen by the project manager.

220. Answer: D.
PMBOK® Guide, page 521, Section 13.2.2.5

Data Representation
Stakeholder engagement assessment matrix.
A stakeholder engagement assessment matrix supports comparison between the current engagement levels of stakeholders and the desired engagement levels required for successful project delivery. One way to classify the engagement level of stakeholders is shown in Figure 13-6. The engagement level of stakeholders can be classified as follows:
- **Unaware.** Unaware of the project and potential impacts.
- **Resistant.** Aware of the project and potential impacts, but resistant to any changes that may occur as a result of the work or outcomes of the project. These stakeholders will be unsupportive of the work or outcomes of the project.
- **Neutral.** Aware of the project, but neither supportive nor unsupportive.
- **Supportive.** Aware of the project and potential impacts, and supportive of the work and its outcomes.
- **Leading.** Aware of the project and potential impacts, and actively engaged in ensuring that the project is a success.

221. Answer: B.
PMBOK® Guide, page 523, Section 13.3

Manage Stakeholder Engagement
Manage Stakeholder Engagement is the process of communicating and working with stakeholders to meet their needs and expectations, address issues, and foster appropriate stakeholder involvement. The key benefit of this process is that it allows the project manager to increase support and minimize resistance from stakeholders. This process is performed throughout the project. The inputs, tools and techniques, and outputs of the process are depicted in Figure 13-7. Figure 13-8 depicts the data flow diagram for the process.

222. Answer: C.
PMBOK® Guide, page 523, Section 13.3

Manage Stakeholder Engagement
Manage Stakeholder Engagement is the process of communicating and working with stakeholders to meet their needs and expectations, address issues, and foster appropriate stakeholder involvement. The key benefit of this process is that it allows the project manager to increase support and minimize resistance from stakeholders. This process is performed throughout the project. The inputs, tools and techniques, and outputs of the process are depicted in Figure 13-7. Figure 13-8 depicts the data flow diagram for the process.

The ability of stakeholders to influence the project is typically highest during the initial stages and gets progressively lower as the project progresses. The project manager is responsible for engaging and managing the various stakeholders in a project and may call upon the project sponsor to assist as needed. Active management of stakeholder involvement decreases the risk of the project failing to meet its goals and objectives.

223. Answer: D.
PMBOK® Guide, pages 533–534, Section 13.4.2

The Monitor Stakeholder Engagement process has the following tools and techniques:
.1 Data analysis
- Alternatives analysis
- Root cause analysis
- Stakeholder analysis
- Stakeholder engagement assessment matrix
.2 Decision making
- Multicriteria decision analysis
- Voting
.3 Meetings
.4 Communication
- Feedback
- Presentations and other verbal communications
- Stakeholder mapping/representation
.5 Interpersonal and team skills
- Active listening
- Cultural awareness

224. Answer: B.
PMBOK® Guide, page 512, Section 13.1.2.4

Data Representation
Power/interest grid, power/influence grid, or impact/influence grid. Each of these techniques supports a grouping of stakeholders according to their level of authority (power), level of concern about the project's outcomes (interest), ability to influence the outcomes of the project (influence), or ability to cause changes to the project's planning or execution. These classification models are useful for small projects or for projects with simple relationships between stakeholders and the project, or within the stakeholder community itself.

225. Answer: C.

PMBOK® Guide, pages 512–513, Section 13.1.2.4

Data Representation

A data representation technique that may be used in this process includes, but is not limited to, stakeholder mapping/representation. Stakeholder mapping and representation is a method of categorizing stakeholders using various methods. Categorizing stakeholders assists the team in building relationships with the identified project stakeholders. Common methods include the following:

- **Power/interest grid, power/influence grid, or impact/influence grid.** Each of these techniques supports a grouping of stakeholders according to their level of authority (power), level of concern about the project's outcomes (interest), ability to influence the outcomes of the project (influence), or ability to cause changes to the project's planning or execution. These classification models are useful for small projects or for projects with simple relationships between stakeholders and the project, or within the stakeholder community itself.
- **Stakeholder cube.** This is a refinement of the grid models previously mentioned. This model combines the grid elements into a three-dimensional model that can be useful to project managers and teams in identifying and engaging their stakeholder community. It provides a model with multiple dimensions that improves the depiction of the stakeholder community as a multidimensional entity and assists with the development of communication strategies.
- **Salience model.** This model describes classes of stakeholders based on assessments of their power (level of authority or ability to influence the outcomes of the project), urgency (need for immediate attention, either time-constrained or relating to the stakeholder's high stake in the outcome), and legitimacy (their involvement is appropriate). There is an adaptation of the salience model that substitutes proximity for legitimacy (applying to the team and measuring their level

of involvement with the work of the project). The salience model is most useful for large, complex communities of stakeholders or where there are complex networks of relationships within the community. It is also useful in determining the relative importance of the identified stakeholders.

- **Directions of influence.** This classifies stakeholders according to their influence on the work of the project or the project team itself.

226. Answer: C.
PMBOK® Guide, page 530, Section 13.4, Figure 13-9

Monitor Stakeholder Engagement
Monitor Stakeholder Engagement is the process of monitoring project stakeholder relationships and tailoring strategies for engaging stakeholders through modification of engagement strategies and plans. The key benefit of this process is that it maintains or increases the efficiency and effectiveness of stakeholder engagement activities as the project evolves and its environment changes. This process is performed throughout the project. The inputs, tools and techniques, and outputs of the process are depicted in Figure 13-9.

Appendix X3
(Agile, Iterative, Adaptive, and Hybrid Project Environments)

227. Answer: C.
PMBOK® Guide, page 665, Section X3.1

The Continuum of Project Life Cycles
To understand the application of the process in adaptive projects, the continuum of project life cycles should be defined. The *PMBOK® Guide* Glossary describes the project life cycle as "the series of phases that a project passes through from its start to its completion." Within a project life cycle, there are generally one or more phases that are associated with the development of the product, service, or result. These are called a development life cycle. Development life cycles can be predictive (plan-driven), adaptive (agile), iterative, incremental, or a hybrid.

228. Answer: A.
PMBOK® Guide, page 667, Section X3.2.1

Sequential Iteration-Based Phases
Adaptive projects are often decomposed into a sequence of phases called iterations. Each iteration utilizes the relevant project management processes. These iterations create a cadence of predictable, time-boxed, pre-agreed, consistent duration that aids with scheduling.

Performing the Process Groups repeatedly incurs overhead. The overhead is considered necessary to effectively manage projects with high degrees of complexity, uncertainty, and change. The effort level for iteration-based phases is illustrated in Figure X3-2.

Section X3.2.2 Continuous Overlapping Phases
Projects that are highly adaptive will often perform all of the Project Management Process Groups continuously throughout the project life cycle. Inspired by techniques from lean thinking, the adaptive approach is often referred to as "continuous and adaptive planning," which acknowledges that once work starts, the plan will change, and the plan needs to reflect this new knowledge. The intent is to aggressively refine and improve all elements of the project management plan, beyond the prescheduled checkpoints associated with Iterations. The interaction of the Process Groups in this approach is illustrated in Figure X3-3.

Figure X3-3: Relationship of Process Groups in Continuous Phases

These highly adaptive approaches continuously pull tasks from a prioritized list of work. This aims to minimize the overhead of managing Process Groups repeatedly, by removing the start and end of iteration activities. Continuous pull systems can be viewed as micro-iterations with an emphasis on maximizing the time available on execution rather than management. They do, however, need their own planning, tracking, and adjustment mechanisms to keep them on track and adapt to changes.

229. Answer: C.
PMBOK® Guide, page 668, Section X3.2.2

> Scope Management is not a Process Group in an adaptive environment.
> Section X3.3.1 Initiating Process Group
> Section X3.3.2 Planning Process Group
> Section X3.3.3 Executing Process Group
> Section X3.3.4 Monitoring and Controlling Process Group
> Section X3.3.5 Closing Process Group

230. Answer: B.
PMBOK® Guide, page 671, Section X3.2.4

Monitoring and Controlling Process Group
Monitoring and Controlling processes are those processes required to track, review, and regulate the progress and performance of the project; identify any areas in which changes to the plan are required; and initiate the corresponding changes.

Iterative, agile, and adaptive approaches track, review, and regulate progress and performance by *maintaining a backlog*. The backlog is prioritized by a business representative, with help from the project team, who estimates and provides information about technical dependencies. Work is pulled from the top of the backlog for the next iteration based on business priority and team capacity. Requests for change and defect reports are evaluated by the business representative in consultation with the team for technical input and are prioritized accordingly in the backlog of work.

31. Answer: B.

PMBOK® Guide, page 669, Section X3.3.2

Planning Process Group

Planning processes are those processes required to establish the scope of the project, refine the objectives, and define the course of action required to attain the objectives that the project was undertaken to achieve. Highly predictive project life cycles are generally characterized by few changes to project scope and high stakeholder alignment. These projects benefit from detailed up-front planning. Adaptive life cycles, on the other hand, develop a set of high-level plans for the initial requirements and progressively elaborate requirements to an appropriate level of detail for the planning cycle. Therefore, predictive and adaptive life cycles differ as to how much planning is done and when it is done.

Appendix X4
(Summary of Key Concepts for Knowledge Areas)

232. Answer: A.
PMBOK® Guide, page 673, Section X4.1

Key concepts for Project Integration Management include Project Integration Management is the specific responsibility of the project manager and it cannot be delegated or transferred. The project manager combines the results from all the other Knowledge Areas to provide an overall view of the project. It is the project manager who is ultimately responsible for the project.

Projects and project management are integrative by nature, with most tasks involving more than one Knowledge Area.

The relationships of processes within the Project Management Process Groups and between the Project Management Process Groups are iterative.

Project Integration Management is about:
- Ensuring that the due dates of project deliverables, the project life cycle, and the benefits realization plan are aligned;
- Providing a project management plan to achieve the project objectives;
- Ensuring the creation and use of appropriate knowledge to and from the project;
- Managing project performance and changes to the project activities;
- Measuring and monitoring progress and taking appropriate action;
- Collecting, analyzing, and communicating project information to relevant stakeholders;
- Managing phase transitions when necessary; and
- Completing all the work of the project and formally closing each phase, contract, and the project as a whole.

233. Answer: B.
PMBOK® Guide, page 674, Section X4.2

Key concepts for Project Scope Management include:
- Scope can refer to product scope (the features and functions that characterize a product, service, or result), or to project scope (the work performed to deliver a product, service, or result with the specified features and functions).
- Project life cycles range along a continuum from predictive to adaptive or agile. In a life cycle that uses a predictive approach, the project deliverables are defined at the beginning of the project and any changes to the scope are progressively managed. In an adaptive or agile approach, the deliverables are developed over multiple iterations where a detailed scope is defined and approved for each iteration when it begins.
- Completion of the project scope is measured against the project management plan. Completion of the product scope is measured against the product requirements.

234. Answer: C.
PMBOK® Guide, page 674, Section X4.3

Key concepts for Project Schedule Management include:
- Project scheduling provides a detailed plan that represents how and when the project will deliver the products, services, and results defined in the project scope;
- The project schedule is used as a tool for communication, managing stakeholder expectations, and a basis for performance reporting; and
- When possible, the detailed project schedule should remain flexible throughout the project to adjust for knowledge gained, increased understanding of the risk, and value-added activities.

235. Answer: D.

PMBOK® Guide, page 674, Section X4.4

Key concepts for Project Cost Management include the following:
- Project Cost Management is primarily concerned with the cost of the resources needed to complete project activities, but it should also consider the effect of project decisions on the subsequent recurring cost of using, maintaining, and supporting project deliverables.
- Different stakeholders will measure project costs in different ways and at different times. Stakeholder requirements for managing costs should be considered explicitly.
- Predicting and analyzing the prospective financial performance of the project's product may be performed outside the project, or it may be part of Project Cost Management.

Key concepts for Project Quality Management include:

- Project Quality Management addresses the management of the project and the deliverables of the project. It applies to all projects, regardless of the nature of their deliverables. Quality measures and techniques are specific to the type of deliverables being produced by the project.

- Quality and grade are different concepts. Quality is "the degree to which a set of inherent characteristics fulfills requirements" (ISO 9000). Grade is a category assigned to deliverables having the same functional use but different technical characteristics. The project manager and team are responsible for managing trade-offs associated with delivering the required levels of both quality and grade.

- Prevention is preferred over inspection. It is better to design quality into deliverables, rather than to find quality issues during inspection. The cost of preventing mistakes is generally much less than the cost of correcting mistakes when they are found by inspection or during usage.

- Project managers may need to be familiar with sampling, including attribute sampling (the result either conforms or does not conform) and variable sampling (the result is rated on a continuous scale that measures the degree of conformity).

- Many projects establish tolerances and control limits for project and product measurements. Tolerances (the specified range of acceptable results) and control limits (the boundaries of common variation in a statistically stable process or process performance).

- The cost of quality (COQ) includes all costs incurred over the life of the product by investment in preventing nonconformance to requirements, appraising the product or service for conformance to requirements, and failing to meet requirements (rework). Cost of quality is often the concern of portfolio management, program management, the PMO, or operations.
- The most effective quality management is achieved when quality is incorporated into the planning and designing of the project and product, and when organizational culture is aware of and committed to quality.

37. Answer: B.

PMBOK® Guide, page 676, Section X4.6

Key concepts for Project Resource Management include the following:

- Project resources include both physical resources (equipment, materials, facilities, and infrastructure) and team resources (individuals with assigned project roles and responsibilities).
- Different skills and competences are needed to manage team resources versus physical resources.
- The project manager should be both the leader and the manager of the project team, and should invest suitable effort in acquiring, managing, motivating, and empowering team members.
- The project manager should be aware of team influences such as the team environment, geographical location of team members, communication among stakeholders, organizational change management, internal and external politics, cultural issues, and organizational uniqueness.
- The project manager is responsible for proactively developing team skills and competences while retaining and improving team satisfaction and motivation.
- Physical resource management is concentrated on allocating and utilizing the physical resources needed for successful completion of the project in an efficient and effective way. Failure to manage and control resources efficiently may reduce the chance of completing the project successfully.

238. Answer: C.

PMBOK® Guide, pages 676–677, Section X4.7

Key concepts for Project Communications Management include the following:

- Communication is the process of exchanging information, intended or involuntary, between individuals and/or groups. Communications describes the means by which information can be sent or received, either through activities, such as meetings and presentations, or artifacts, such as emails, social media, project reports, or project documentation. Project Communications Management addresses both the process of communication and management of communications activities and artifacts.

- Effective communication creates a bridge between diverse stakeholders whose differences will generally have an impact or influence upon the project execution or outcome, so it is vital that all communication is clear and concise.

- Communication activities include internal and external, formal and informal, and written and oral forms of communication.

- Communication can be directed upward to senior management stakeholders, downward to team members, or horizontally to peers. This will affect the format and content of the message.

- Communication takes place consciously or unconsciously through words, facial expressions, gestures, and other actions. It includes developing strategies and plans for suitable communications artifacts, and the application of skills to enhance effectiveness.

- Effort is required to prevent misunderstandings and miscommunication, and the methods, messengers, and messages should be carefully selected.

- Effective communication depends on defining the purpose of communication, understanding the receiver of the communications, and monitoring effectiveness.

239. Answer: D.

PMBOK® Guide, page 677, Section X4.8

Key concepts for Project Risk Management include the following:

- All projects are risky. Organizations choose to take project risk in order to create value, while balancing risk and reward.
- Project Risk Management aims to identify and manage risks that are not covered by other project management processes.
- Risk exists at two levels within every project: Individual project risk is an uncertain event or condition that, if it occurs, has a positive or negative effect on one or more project objectives. Overall project risk is the effect of uncertainty on the project as a whole, arising from all sources of uncertainty, including individual risks, representing the exposure of stakeholders to the implications of variations in project outcome, both positive and negative. Project Risk Management processes address both levels of risk in projects.
- Individual project risks can have a positive or negative effect on project objectives if they occur. Overall project risk can also be positive or negative.
- Risks will continue to emerge during the lifetime of the project, so Project Risk Management processes should be conducted iteratively.
- In order to manage risk effectively on a particular project, the project team needs to know what level of risk exposure is acceptable in pursuit of project objectives. This is defined by measurable risk thresholds that reflect the risk appetite of the organization and project stakeholders.

240. Answer: A.

PMBOK® Guide, page 678, Section X4.9

Key concepts for Project Procurement Management include the following:

- The project manager should be familiar enough with the procurement process to make intelligent decisions regarding contracts and contractual relationships.
- Procurement involves agreements that describe the relationship between a buyer and a seller. Agreements can be simple or complex, and the procurement approach should reflect the degree of complexity. An agreement can be a contract, a service-level agreement, an understanding, a memorandum of agreement, or a purchase order.
- Agreements must comply with local, national, and international laws regarding contracts.
- The project manager should ensure that all procurements meet the specific needs of the project, while working with procurement specialists to ensure that organizational policies are followed.
- The legally binding nature of an agreement means it will be subjected to a more extensive approval process, often involving the legal department, to ensure that it adequately describes the products, services, or results that the seller is agreeing to provide, while being in compliance with the laws and regulations regarding procurements.
- A complex project may involve multiple contracts simultaneously or in sequence. The buyer-seller relationship may exist at many levels on any one project, and between organizations internal to and external to the acquiring organization.

241. Answer: B.

PMBOK® Guide, page 678, Section X4.10

Key concepts for Project Stakeholder Management include the following:

- Every project has stakeholders who are impacted by, or can impact, the project in a positive or negative way. Some stakeholders will have a limited ability to influence the project's work or outcomes; others will have significant influence on the project and its expected outcomes.
- The ability of the project manager and team to correctly identify and engage all of the stakeholders in an appropriate way can mean the difference between project success and failure.
- To increase the chances of success, the process of stakeholder identification and engagement should commence as soon as possible after the project charter has been approved, the project manager has been assigned, and the team begins to form.
- The key to effective stakeholder engagement is a focus on continuous communication with all stakeholders. Stakeholder satisfaction should be identified and managed as a key project objective.
- The process of identifying and engaging stakeholders for the benefit of the project is iterative, and should be reviewed and updated routinely, particularly when the project moves into a new phase, or if there are significant changes in the organization or the wider stakeholder community.

Appendix X5

242. Answer: D.

PMBOK® Guide, page 680, Section X5.3

Project Schedule Management

According to the *PMBOK® Guide* – Sixth Edition, governance is typically tailored in the Project Scope Management Knowledge Area, and not recognized as a Knowledge Area to be tailored in the Project Schedule Management phase. Definitions of the following are below.

- **Life cycle approach.** What is the most appropriate life cycle approach that allows for a detailed schedule?
- **Duration and resource.** What are the factors influencing durations, such as the correlation between resource availability and productivity?
- **Project dimensions.** How will the presence of project complexity, technological uncertainty, product novelty, and pace or progress tracking (such as earned value management, percentage complete, red-yellow-green [stop light] indicators) impact the desired level of control?
- **Technology support.** Is technology used to develop, record, transmit, receive, and store project schedule model information and is it readily accessible?

243. Answer: C.

PMBOK® Guide, page 681, Section X5.5

Project Quality Management

- **Stakeholder engagement.** Is there a collaborative environment with stakeholders and suppliers?
- **Policy compliance and auditing.** What quality policies and procedures exist in the organization? What quality tools, techniques, and templates are used in the organization?
- **Project complexity, uncertainty, product novelty.** These are important concepts in project management; however, they are not typically tailored.
- **Standards and regulatory compliance.** Are there any specific quality standards in the industry that need to be applied? Are there any specific governmental, legal, or regulatory constraints that need to be taken into consideration?

244. Answer: C.

PMBOK® Guide, page 682, Section X5.6

Project Resource Management

- **Diversity.** What is the diversity background of the team?
- **Physical location.** What is the physical location of team members and physical resources?
- **Number of team members.** The number of team members should always reflect the overall work that needs to be completed in order to meet the project objectives. It is not a primary focus of tailoring activities.
- **Life cycle approaches.** What life cycle approach will be used on the project?

245. Answer: D.

PMBOK® Guide, page 683, Section X5.8

Project Risk Management
- **Project complexity.** Is a robust risk approach demanded by high levels of innovation, new technology, commercial arrangements, interfaces, or external dependencies that increase project complexity? Or is the project simple enough that a reduced risk process will suffice?
- **Project importance.** How strategically important is the project? Is the level of risk increased for this project because it aims to produce breakthrough opportunities, addresses significant blocks to organizational performance, or involves major product innovation?
- **Project size.** Does the project's size in terms of budget, duration, scope, or team size require a more detailed approach to risk management? Or is it small enough to justify a simplified risk process?
- **Project duration.** This is not a concept which would be under consideration for tailoring in risk management.

46. Answer: D.
PMBOK® Guide, page 684, Section X5.10

Project Stakeholder Management
- **Complexity of stakeholder relationships.**
  How complex are the relationships within the
  stakeholder community? The more networks a
  stakeholder or stakeholder group participates in,
  the more complex the networks of information
  and misinformation the stakeholder may receive.
- **Stakeholder diversity.** How many stakeholders
  are there? How diverse is the culture within the
  stakeholder community?
- **Communication technology.** What communication
  technology is available? What support mechanisms
  are in place to ensure that best value is achieved from
  the technology?
- **Stakeholder engagement.** This is the process of
  communicating and working with stakeholders to
  meet their needs and expectations, address issues,
  and foster appropriate stakeholder involvement.

247. Answer: D.
PMBOK® Guide, page 681, Section X5.4

Project Cost Management
- **Estimating and budgeting.** Does the organization
  have existing formal or informal cost estimating
  and budgeting-related policies, procedures, and
  guidelines?
- **Earned value management.** Does the
  organization use earned value management in
  managing projects?
- **Governance.** Does the organization have formal
  or informal audit and governance policies,
  procedures, and guidelines?
- **Continuous improvement.** How will quality
  improvement be managed in the project? Is it
  managed at the organizational level or at the level
  of each project? This is considered for tailoring
  under the Project Quality Management process.

Glossary

248. Answer: A.
PMBOK® Guide, page 199, Section 6.4.1.2; and Glossary

> **Resource requirements.** The types and quantities of resources required for each activity in a work package

249. Answer: B.
PMBOK® Guide, page 19, Section 1.2.4.1; and Glossary

> **Adaptive life cycle.** A project life cycle that is iterative or incremental.

250. Answer: C.
PMBOK® Guide, page 200, Section 6.4.2.2; and Glossary

> **Analogous estimating.** A technique for estimating the duration or cost of an activity or a project using historical data from a similar activity or project.

251. Answer: D.
PMBOK® Guide, Glossary

> **Assumption.** A factor in the planning process that is considered to be true, real, or certain, without proof or demonstration.

252. Answer: A.
PMBOK® Guide, page 204, Section 6.4.3.2; and Glossary

> **Basis of estimates.** Supporting documentation outlining the details used in establishing project estimates such as assumptions, constraints, level of detail, ranges, and confidence levels.

253. Answer: B.
PMBOK® Guide, page 30, Section 1.2.6.1; and Glossary

Business case. A documented economic feasibility study used to establish validity of the benefits of a selected component lacking sufficient definition and that is used as a basis for the authorization of further project management activities.

254. Answer: C.
PMBOK® Guide, Glossary

Checklist analysis. A technique for systematically reviewing materials using a list for accuracy and completeness.

255. Answer: D.
PMBOK® Guide, pages 369–370, Section 10.1.2.2; and Glossary

Communication requirements analysis. An analytical technique to determine the information needs of the project stakeholders through interviews, workshops, study of lessons learned from previous projects, etc.

256. Answer: B.
PMBOK® Guide, page 245, Section 7.2.2.6; and Glossary

Contingency reserve. Time or money allocated in the schedule or cost baseline for known risks with active response strategies.

257. Answer: C.
PMBOK® Guide, page 282, Section 8.1.2.3; and Glossary

Cost of quality (CoQ). All costs incurred over the life of the product by investment in preventing nonconformance to requirements, appraisal of the product or service for conformance to requirements, and failure to meet requirements.

258. Answer: C.

PMBOK® Guide, Glossary

Critical path activity. Any activity on the critical path in a project schedule.

259. Answer: D.

PMBOK® Guide, page 191, Section 6.3.2.2; and Glossary

Total float. The amount of time that a schedule activity can be delayed or extended from its early start date without delaying the project finish date or violating a schedule constraint.

260. Answer: A.

PMBOK® Guide, page 19, Section 1.2.4.1; and Glossary

Incremental life cycle. An adaptive project life cycle in which the deliverable is produced through a series of iterations that successively add functionality within a predetermined time frame. The deliverable contains the necessary and sufficient capability to be considered complete only after the final iteration.

261. Answer: B.

PMBOK® Guide, page 19, Section 1.2.4.1; and Glossary

Iterative life cycle. An adaptive project life cycle in which the deliverable matures through a series of repeated cycles. The deliverable contains the necessary and sufficient capability to be considered complete at the end of each cycle. Each repeated cycle further enhances the capability of the deliverable.

62. Answer: C.

PMBOK® Guide, page 19, Section 1.2.4.1; and Glossary

> **Predictive life cycle.** A form of project life cycle in which the project scope, time, and cost are determined in the early phases of the life cycle.

63. Answer: D.

PMBOK® Guide, page 185, Section 6.2.2.3; and Glossary

> **Progressive elaboration.** The iterative process of increasing the level of detail in a project management plan as greater amounts of information and more accurate estimates become available.

64. Answer: A.

PMBOK® Guide, page 290, Section 8.2; and Glossary

> **Quality audits.** A quality audit is a structured, independent process to determine if project activities comply with organizational and project policies, processes, and procedures.

65. Answer: B.

PMBOK® Guide, page 317, Section 9.1.2.2; and Glossary

> **RACI chart.** A common type of responsibility assignment matrix that uses responsible, accountable, consult, and inform statuses to define the involvement of stakeholders in project activities.

66. Answer: C.

PMBOK® Guide, page 325, Section 9.2.3.1; and Glossary

> **Requirements documentation.** A description of how individual requirements meet the business need for the project.

267. Answer: D.
PMBOK® Guide, page 448, Section 11.5.3.3; and Glossary

Residual risk. The risk that remains after risk responses have been implemented.

268. Answer: A.
PMBOK® Guide, page 211, Section 6.5.2.3; and Glossary

Resource leveling. A resource optimization technique in which adjustments are made to the project schedule to optimize the allocation of resources and which may affect critical path. See also resource optimization technique and resource smoothing.

269. Answer: B.
PMBOK® Guide, page 185, Section 6.2.2.3; and Glossary

Rolling wave planning. An iterative planning technique in which the work to be accomplished in the near term is planned in detail, while the work in the future is planned at a higher level.

270. Answer: C.
PMBOK® Guide, page 254, Section 7.3.3.1; and Glossary

Cost baseline. The approved version of the time-phased project budget, excluding any management reserves, which can be changed only through formal change control procedures and is used as a basis for comparison to actual results.

271. Answer: D.

PMBOK® Guide, page 161, Section 5.4.3.1; and Glossary

> **Scope baseline.** The approved version of a scope
> statement, work breakdown structure (WBS), and its
> associated WBS dictionary, that can be changed using
> formal change control procedures and is used as a
> basis for comparison to actual results.

272. Answer: A.

PMBOK® Guide, page 478, Section 12.1.3.5; and Glossary

> **Source selection criteria.** A set of attributes desired
> by the buyer that a seller is required to meet or exceed
> to be selected for a contract.

273. Answer: B.

PMBOK® Guide, page 477, Section 12.1.3.4; and Glossary

> **Statement of work (SOW).** A narrative description
> of products, services, or results to be delivered by the
> project.

274. Answer: C.

PMBOK® Guide, page 28, Section 1.2.5; and Glossary

> **Tailoring.** Determining the appropriate combination
> of processes, inputs, tools, techniques, outputs, and
> life cycle phases to manage a project.

275. Answer: D.

PMBOK® Guide, page 296, Section 8.2.3.2; and Glossary

> **Test and evaluation documents.** Project documents
> that describe the activities used to determine if the
> product meets the quality objectives stated in the
> quality management plan.

276. Answer: A.
PMBOK® Guide, page 570, Section 3; and Glossary

> **Work breakdown structure (WBS).** A hierarchical decomposition of the total scope of work to be carried out by the project team to accomplish the project objectives and create the required deliverables.

277. Answer: B.
PMBOK® Guide, page 161, Section 5.4.3.1; and Glossary

> **Work package.** The work defined at the lowest level of the work breakdown structure for which cost and duration are estimated and managed.